I AM
NOT
YVONNE
NELSON

YVONNE NELSON

ISBN : 978 - 9988 - 3 - 5665 - 1

Editing and proofreading:
Mavis Donkor
Elizabeth Borteye

Cover photograph: Courage Xah

Cover design: Lamptey Desmond Adu Boahen

Layout: Sirlaud Mimaose

Printed: Marcel Hughes

Published By: Yvonne Nelson Studios

Contacts of the author:
Email: iamnotyvonnenelson@gmail.com
Facebook: YVONNE NELSON
Twitter: @yvonnenelsongh
Instagram: @yvonnenelsongh
Telephone: +233509993939

1

DEDICATION

This book is dedicated to Ryn Nelson Roberts. Thank you for giving me a purpose in life.

FOREWORD

The legendary Nigerian writer, Chinua Achebe, once said, "If you don't like someone's story, write your own." Writing one's own story helps to cure the misrepresentation and inaccuracies that are likely to occur if one's story is told by others. However, writing one's story does not come easy. Anyone who decides to write his or her own story is often confronted with the dilemma of how far to go, how much to reveal, and how clean the writer should look in the story.

In most cases, such stories come out with exaggerated virtues of the writer. The rough edges are often trimmed, and all the creases about their lives are neatly ironed out, leaving an almost perfect account of an obviously imperfect person.

In this book, however, Yvonne Nelson has decided to be different. With a special kind of boldness, she has opened the door into her life without first cleaning up the messy aspects of it. It's like waking up and posing for the camera without any makeup on. Considering the society in which the author operates and is familiar with, it is a rare act of bravery to write the things contained in this book.

This book is not an ordinary autobiography. It is a search for an answer to a question that has nagged the author since her childhood. It chronicles a journey that starts unassumingly but auspiciously in Dansoman, gets gloomy and bleak after Aggrey Memorial AME Zion Secondary School in Cape Coast, and sets the stage for the author's struggles; a struggle against failure and the desertion that comes with it, a struggle which later becomes the fight against the pitfalls of fame and success.

In essence, this book recounts an endless struggle by the author to discover herself and her place in the world. She faces a fair dose of ups and downs. As with all human stories, there are surprises and dramatic ironies that are known, perhaps, only to Providence. For instance, Aggrey Memorial, which she despises so much turns out to be the right place that prepares her for the success that would define her life.

In the midst of the struggle for success and against the battles that come with it is the bigger and overriding theme of the story. It begins on the first page and ends on the last—the mystery about the author's father. This story has almost all the elements of fiction. However, the major conflict of the story remains unresolved as the reader closes the pages and wonders what is next.

Those whose perception of celebrities is defined by glittery photographs on glossy magazine covers with stories that contain glossier portrayals of the celebrities' lives will find this book revealing, if not shocking. It lays bare the struggles and failures and fears of the men and women who, at some point or the other, own the screens of our television sets. This book also gives an insider's perspective of female celebrities and settles the debate about whether sex-for-roles in the movie industry is a perception or reality, at least in Nigeria and Ghana.

Above all, it also subtly reveals the power celebrities wield. The success story of the author's protest against Ghana's power crisis in 2015 and the visit by President Akufo-Addo's close associate to convince her to contest a parliamentary seat on the ticket of the NPP in 2020 attest to the power celebrities wield beyond the entertainment circles.

This is a book that is bound to ruffle feathers and ignite wild debates, but those who read it objectively and without the judgmental binoculars will see the story of a young woman—fallible like all other mortals—who is determined to leave a mark despite the internal and external forces that have erected high hurdles in her way.

Manasseh Azure Awuni
(Ghanaian Journalist and Author)
April 2023

A WORD FROM
THE AUTHOR

Life, they say, begins at 40. This saying is rooted in the belief that, by a person's fourth decade on earth, he or she should have laid the foundations necessary for a smooth and more rewarding take-off into the next half of his or her existence on earth. If this saying is anything to go by, then my life is yet to begin. I will be 38 in November; and per the constitution of Ghana, no person below 40 years is eligible to be elected president of the country, even if he or she is able to carry the entire nation to the moon and back.

So why am I in a hurry to write my memoir before I turn 40? Do I think I have achieved so much that this stage of my life deserves a book? Have I reached the pinnacle of my goals and ambitions?

I have covered quite a distance, but what I envisage before me is more ambitious than what is behind me. So, I am not writing this because

I think I have peaked. It is said that a person's speed in the battle of life is determined by the speed of his or her pursuer. That which is determining the speed of my run started its vicious and supersonic pursuit before I was born. I have been running in silence, apart from a few hints I have dropped here and there in some major media interviews.

Some people, mainly bloggers and reporters in the entertainment industry, have tried to take the disjointed bits and pieces and weave their own stories about my life. They have tried to convince their audience that their version of my story is the one and only definitive account. Some of those strange stories sound like works of fiction grounded in real-life scenarios, at least with a real character. I have engaged in some firefighting in the past, trying without much success, to extinguish some flames of untruths, half-truths and outright misinformation.

Correcting other people's accounts of me is, however, not the reason I am telling my own story at this stage. I am not here to seek sympathy or validation. I am not here to challenge anyone's version or correct anyone's narrative.

I am writing because I have a story to tell. I am here to be real. I am here to open up, especially to a generation of young women that needs the truth to make decisions. I am here to find the most important answer to the most nagging question about my life.

I was barely out of my teen years when fate thrust me in a career that makes the limelight inevitable. Being in that limelight comes with its own etiquettes. You are required to conform to the etiquettes and swim along the tide. You are expected to move with the flow, even if it runs counter to your reality.

Being called a celebrity is a bestowment of a package on you. It sometimes comes with unrealistic demands and expectations. You have to live for the people. You have to learn the celebratory cues and act on them as if your very existence depended on them. Your reality does not matter if it does not align with the make-believe reality of show business. The industry requires one to act out one's real life in much the same way a script containing someone's imagination should be acted out. You have to always smile to the lenses of the prying crowd. You have to conceal your weaknesses. You have to hide your tears and fears.

But there comes a time one finds truer meaning to life, a calling and a cause more fulfilling than the real and imaginary applauses in the market square of stardom. There comes a time one has to be real with oneself. There comes a time when one feels compelled to let the world into one's life and show them the other side, the real side. This, I feel, is my time.

In so doing, I intend to help future generations of young women that are hungry for fame and would do anything to make a name. I do not intend to decide for them or dissuade them from following their dreams. I intend to show them the whole picture. I intend to give them the ingredients to prepare their own meals of life.

I intend to show them the human side of celebrity life. I intend to show them that celebrities are nowhere near the status of superhuman species. Behind the expensive make-up, glittering edited photos and enhanced videos are human beings who have blemishes—physical and emotional— just like everyone else. They have their weaknesses, their fears and disappointments, just like everyone else. It is true that a female celebrity will likely have teeming men, known and unknown men, dying to get her attention. But it is also true that she, too, struggles to get the attention of the man she loves, who may not love her back.

I intend to show young women entering the movie or showbiz industry that they have hard choices to make. They have to choose between growing organically with dignity or leapfrogging into overnight stardom with unspeakable compromises. I intend to show them that they will suffer for their stubborn refusal to earn a place on the big stage with their body.

In telling my story, I have made the hard decision not to sanitise it. I have told it in its raw form. Knowing my society and the high "moral" standard by which its women are measured, it is like taking an uninsurable risk in an already perilous endeavour. However, I want whoever looks up to me to see the whole package. I have had my low and my high moments. I have done things that I'm proud of and things

I could never talk openly about until I decided to write this book. I have run and completed some races. In others, I have faltered and crashed. All of that has shaped me and made me the woman I am. I intend to show those who look up to me the scars of my falls, with the hope that they may avoid the landmines that nearly ended my life.

Above all, the main reason I decided to write this book precedes my birth. I have searched in all the possible places for answers but failed. So, I am telling this story with the hope that I will find answers that will stop the tears that only my pillow can adequately bear witness to.

I am telling my story to discover myself.

Yvonne Nelson
April 2023

CONTENTS

PART ONE

A GIRL WITH A
DOUBTFUL IDENTITY

CHAPTER ONE

A Teacher's Question

What turned out later to be a frantic search and a lifelong fight for my true identity began rather nonchalantly. The trigger was a simple question from a teacher who wanted to cure his casual curiosity. It was a question whose answer I thought I knew without having to scratch my young head, but I ended up racking my adult brain for years, employing scientific methods, and conducting my own investigations but without the corresponding reward for the effort. Every now and then, different variations of that question return to haunt me like a horrifying ghost.

I grew up with a void in my life, but it really didn't mean much to me until that fateful afternoon when my Primary Five class teacher, Mr. B.B. Grant, summoned me to his desk, in front of the classroom. As I approached his desk, another boy in my class also scampered toward us. The teacher had called him too. I did not have the faintest hint about why the two of us were Mr. Grant's subjects of interest and summons, but it would not take forever to find out.

Eugene Nelson was one of the neatest and most handsome boys in the class. As young as he was, he had an aura of respectability around him. Apart from his attitude when provoked, which those in his circles had endured a few times in the past, I could not say anything negative about him. We were not friends. We had our different cliques because our personalities—which were polar opposites—could not contain us in the same group. From afar, I liked Eugene, and that was just it. Even if I had any crush on him, I kept it to myself. To be called to our class teacher's table together, therefore, set me on edge until Mr. Grant spoke.

"Are the two of you related?" he asked.

It was a question that confused me, but Eugene and I did not have any difficulty answering it. We were not related. We bore the same surname, but it wasn't strange to have two or three children in the same class and from different hometowns bearing the same surname. Eugene was short and I was tall. His nose, eyes, head and every other feature of his was different from mine. The only feature we shared was a fair complexion. That, too, was not a novelty, for we were not the only fair children in that class. But the teacher, peering into our personal records on his desk, appeared to know more than we did. To us, we were not related in any way, but he thought there might be something we did not know.

"When you go home, ask your parents," he said and dismissed us.

The teacher's question set me on a lifelong inquest into what has turned out to be the most elusive assignment of my life. The more I discovered, the more I wished the search hadn't started in the first place. But the more answers I got, the more desperate I became about finding the true answer to the most important question of my life—who am I? That I am Yvonne Nelson is a well-established fact to outsiders, but to my family and a handful of friends, I am not Yvonne Nelson. After almost four decades of my existence, I am still as desperate as when that seed of confusion was planted in my head by a teacher who, perhaps, did not appreciate the full import of what he was doing. The search for answers was bound to begin at a certain point in my life, but his question brought some urgency and intensity to the entire enterprise.

The assignment he gave us that day meant different things to Eugene and me. To Eugene, it meant exactly what the teacher said—he should ask his parents. In my case, I had no parents. I had only a parent. Eugene had a father and a mother to ask, but I had only a mother. I would later discover that Eugene, like me, had actually only one parent who was in the position to know the answer.

Assignments from teachers, or what we often called "homework", were supposed to be done at home. If we had a favourite programme on television or an important outing and didn't want the assignment to interfere with our programme, we squeezed some time and did it in school so our day and night would be cleared for our personal stuff. The teacher's assignment on whether Eugene and I were related was not a conventional assignment, and I did not have anything special to attend to at home, but I could not resist the urge to start it right from school.

I started to scan the features of Eugene critically in order to pick hints of our biological relationship, but there was nothing useful from that exercise. When we closed that day, I continued my investigation by standing at a respectable distance to see the man who picked him up from school. The man came, and he was Mr. Nelson. As I had done in the case of Eugene, I tried to pick out features that would lend credence to a possible relationship between Mr. Nelson and me, but there was none. So, I carried the unresolved puzzle home, with a strong resolve to find an answer.

On my way home that day, the teacher's question weighed heavily on me. What I had not paid attention to started to take centre stage in my life. I was still young, but I was old enough to notice some anomalies in my family. I was awake to the stark and uncomfortable reality that I was the odd child at home. Of the four-member nuclear family in my house, there appeared to be a stronger bond among the first three occupants of that house. I felt like a stranger.

When curiosity had driven me to ask my mother why the name of her popular business was Manovia, she said it represented her name and those of my two siblings. She had coined the name from the

18

beginning, middle and ending of their respective names in order of age—Margaret, Enoch and Sylvia. My mother's name is Margaret, and Enoch and Sylvia are her first and second children. I came last. She responded to my next query with the explanation that I had not been born at the time she established the business. I felt left out, but that was not the only or most obvious difference between my two siblings and me.

At primary six, I was about 12 years old and conscious of a number of things. I was conscious of the fact that my two siblings, Enoch and Sylvia, had a surname that was different from mine. Theirs was Davies. And mine was Nelson. I didn't take the time to know much about Davies, but in those days, I did not need to be told that he was an important somebody in the country. Lt. Col. Joseph Kabu Davies was not only a senior military officer but also someone who appeared influential. I had seen photographs of him with President Ft. Lt. Jerry John Rawlings, and that was enough to tell me his pedigree.

Children of my generation grew up seeing Rawlings as an enigma. He had transitioned from a military ruler to a civilian president, but much of what we heard about him were his exploits as a soldier. He was a symbol of bravery, justice and fearlessness. His looks endeared him to many, and his antics and showmanship made him a delight to watch anytime he was on television. As far as some of us were concerned, he was among the most powerful men on earth, and whoever was close to him had to be really important. So, I rated Lt. Col. Davies, the father of my siblings, highly.

When my siblings had once mentioned that my mother was pampering me, I remember her telling them that it was because my father was not there. With that background, the teacher's question ignited in me a fierce determination to know who my father was. I also wanted to know whether the Nelson whose name I carried was the same Nelson who fathered my classmate, Eugene.

My mother is not the type who is used to giving straightforward answers. She prefers to give an explanation before she responds to even close-ended questions. In the case of Mr. Nelson, however, I do not clearly recall the order in which she answered my questions. What I recall was the order in which I processed and stored that information.

I recall her affirmative response to what I considered the most important question of my life. Eugene and I were, indeed, related. The teacher was right. Eugene was my brother. Before I had time to process the revelation and ask further questions, my mother went on to tell me a string of negative tales about Mr. Nelson. These negative stories were part of the reason I never felt emotionally attached to the man whose name I bear. Even if I had any emotional attachment to him, what Mr. Nelson did to me on my first visit to his house was enough to erase it all. That rejection was more painful than being jilted by the most romantic and caring lover.

CHAPTER TWO

A Failed Abortion

I was one of the most popular pupils in one of the most prestigious private basic schools in Ghana at the time, St. Martin de Porres School in Dansoman in Accra. Before a number of more prestigious private schools sprouted everywhere in Ghana, charging fees in American dollars and offering British curricula, St. Martin de Porres School was one of the most exalted schools in the country in the 1990s. That was when private schools were still a preserve of society's privileged, and not the necessity of every parent in today's extremely deteriorated public basic school system.

It was the second private school I attended after a brief spell at a kindergarten that was named after the most popular Catholic figure of my generation—Pope John Paul II, known in private life as Karol Wojtyla. The Pope John Paul Preparatory School collapsed long before Pope John Paul II died in 2005. (That school was situated where the Dansoman Children's Park is today). I cannot say much about its prestige in its heydays, but private schools were not as common then as they are today, and only a few parents could afford to take their children there. So, I assume I started at a good school.

From Pope John Paul Preparatory School, my mother enrolled me in St. Martin de Porres School. The school started in 1973, a dozen years before I was born. With 17 pupils at the beginning, the school now has over 1,200 students and is still regarded as one of the top private schools in Ghana's capital. According to the official history of the school, its founder, Mrs. Florence Laast, named the school after her "favourite saint, Martin de Porres, one of the few black saints in the Catholic faith. He was known for his hard work, humility, and, most of all, his compassion towards his fellowmen."

As I would grow to learn, St. Martin de Porres and what he stood for, perhaps, was more significant to me than it was to the founder of my school. According to Catholic.com, Martin de Porres is a patron saint of Mixed Race, Barbers, Public Health Workers, and Innkeepers. He was beatified in 1837 by Pope Gregory XVI and canonized in 1962 by Pope John XXIII.

According to his official biography, "St. Martin de Porres was born in Lima, Peru on December 9, 1579. Martin was the illegitimate son of a Spanish gentleman and a freed slave from Panama, of African or possibly Native American descent. At a young age, Martin's father abandoned him, his mother and his younger sister, leaving Martin to grow up in deep poverty."

I grew up to learn that I am of a mixed race. I grew up to realise that I was an illegitimate daughter. And until proven otherwise, everything points to the fact that my father abandoned me. Like St. Martin de Porres, I have had my share of ridicule about my parentage. Unlike him, however, I did not grow up in poverty. The fact that I attended St. Martin de Porres School was enough testament to that. It was in this school that I spent at least nine of my formative years, acquiring all that primary and junior high school education had to offer. It was and still is a good school, and I give credit to my mother for giving me a good start in life.

I am still unable to say whether my mother was a rich woman, for my idea of wealth was informed by the affluent families in my neighbourhood, those who lived in bigger houses and drove better cars and went on vacations abroad and did all the things I fantasised about as a child. Looking back, however, I think my mother was not doing badly at all.

We lived in a two-bedroom semi-detached house that had its own spacious compound. It was part of the properly planned and developed Dansoman Estates, which, at one time, boasted of being the largest urban-planned residential area in West Africa. We had two bathrooms with WCs and a kitchen. My mother's business was flourishing, or so I thought, and we did not run out of cash.

23

My mother's shop, Manovia, was the most popular landmark in that part of Dansoman called Sahara. Commuter vehicles used Manovia junction as a bus stop and the nature of the business was such that all manner of persons patronised it. It was a pub and a convenience store. My mother was a distributor of both alcoholic and non-alcoholic drinks. I recall going to the Accra Brewery Limited with my mother, sitting in the car and seeing her supervise the loading of her consignment into delivery vans. I recall seeing her at night counting money with the little bedside lamp she kept by the mirror. She drove her own car and travelled often on business trips. Her busyness with her flourishing business meant that she could not be there for us as she should be. To make up for this, she hired a house-help who took care of us and handled the chores that were above the strength of our feeble hands.

In school, I was popular for a reason most parents at the time would not want their children, especially girls, to be known for—entertainment. I was one of four students who were inspired and influenced by the American hip-hop group, Fugees. Formed in the early 1990s, the group was said to have derived its name from the word "refugees." It is unclear why refugees were of interest to a singing group, but the group's founder, Lauryn Hill, later ventured into a non-profit aimed at helping refugees.

The original Fugees trio had Wyclef Jean, Pras Michel and Lauryn Hill, while the St. Martin de Porres version had Enoch Nana Yaw Oduro- Agyei, Nii Tettey, one Aziz, and me. Being the only female, I was obviously the Lauryn Hill of the group. Nii Tettey had returned from the United States to join us in junior secondary school as it was then called. With his American accent, he was the closest we came to mimicking Fugees. We memorized and sang their songs at school functions. There were times we composed our own songs and performed them at school functions.

As a group, our favourite was Fugees, but my personal favourite was the Ghanaian rapper Obrafour. There was something about his music that blew my mind—the unparalleled depth and the dexterity with which he owned the Twi language in his raps. Obrafour's music was so rich that members of the older generation who were not accustomed to hiplife and rap music got drafted into the genre because of his irresistible appeal. I did not have his photos in my room, but he was permanently engraved in my heart. I was influenced by foreign musicians, but Obrafour has been my all-time greatest singer. I remember how I saved money from my feeding allowance to buy his "Pae Mu Ka" album and learnt every line of each song in that album. He used to come to a studio in Dansoman SSNIT flats—I think it's called DKB Studio or so—and that was the closest I got to seeing him in person. Whenever I spotted him in his short dreadlocks at the time, I would shout his name from my school compound. Many years later, while helping him promote his 20th-anniversary concert, I told Obrafour how I used to shout his name. I didn't know whether he believed it, but he remains my finest artist of all time.

Besides Fugees, my group performed Obrafour's songs in school. He was big in the day and still commands enormous respect in the industry. We dreamt about growing up and sticking together to do great things as a musical group. Life, however, had different plans for us. Our ultimate goal started to dissipate even before we completed basic school. Our circumstances separated us even before we had time to plan how to stick together and pursue that dream.

Aziz is now married with children. Nii Tettey returned to the United States after junior high school and not much is heard about him now. Enoch Yaw Oduro-Agyei is, perhaps, the direct beneficiary of our childhood attempt at music. He is a Ghanaian singer and composer under the stage name Trigmatic. I also ended up in the entertainment industry outside of music, but the influence of American music almost defined my life even before I figured out the course of my young and not-so-ambitious trajectory.

I used to have photos of Fugees in my room, and my family thought I was useless. The whole American music culture influenced me a great deal. I dressed like a boy, and I still have traces of that tomboyish lifestyle in me to date. The influence was huge, and I loved it. But what appeared like a craze for music and the arts was a good escape for me, an escape from loneliness, especially as I began to discover that I didn't fully belong in my family. Music was, therefore, a welcome escape from a possible depression that could have come with that childhood loneliness.

26

My other therapeutic moments were the times I spent with my best friend, Miranda Mould. Miranda had her own share of the weight which life had placed on our young and fragile shoulders. She lived about three blocks from my house and we spent a lot of quality time together.

We often sat near the Ghana Telecom telephone booth that was close to my mother's shop, and whenever it malfunctioned, we served as the prompters to those coming to patronise it. We would tell them it was not functioning and continue with our discussion as they turned away. Sometimes we just sat there, with nothing to talk about but enjoying each other's company while thinking about what preoccupied us at the time. And I had a lot to occupy my mind.

My teacher's question had led me to discover a lot more about myself, most of which were not pleasant. The immediate discovery was about a father who didn't like me, a father who behaved like I did not exist. The story from my mother was not something that could make up for the absence of a father. It was the unflattering story of my birth, which came up a number of times in situations of anger.

When my mother was angry with me and really wanted to hurt me, she would tell me she had given birth to me by mistake. Whenever she said it, she knew how I felt. She knew she was driving a sharp nail into my heart. I could feel she really wanted to hurt me. Maybe, she was just being truthful. By so doing, however, she wounded my spirit, and that unhealable wound served as a constant reminder that all was not well with me. She made me feel terrible about my existence. I cannot imagine ever getting angry with my daughter and telling her that. And I do not think any child, for whatever reason, deserves such psychological torture. But those words and the story that gave credence to their power constantly reminded me that I was neither wanted nor appreciated.

My mother told me that when she got pregnant, she did not want to have me so she went to see a medical doctor to terminate the pregnancy. (My mother has told me that the doctor who saved my life is still alive, but she has not told me who he is or which hospital he worked in.) She took that decision in her sixth month. The doctor agreed, and on the said day, she paid the fees and all was set for the abortion. She lay on the surgical bed, raised her legs, but just when the doctor was about to begin the procedure, he shook his head.

"I can't do this," the doctor told her. "If you really want to do it, go somewhere else. I'm sorry I can't do it."

Gripped by fear and the shock of the doctor's sudden change of mind, she abandoned the idea. But she did not forget how I survived. And she made sure to remind me whenever she felt the need to. It is true that she conceived me by mistake. The details of that story are still too sketchy to be woven into something meaningful. But what is obvious is the fact that I could have ended up as a piece of medical waste if she had made up her mind early enough on whether she wanted to keep me or get rid of me.

I was born on Tuesday, November 12, 1985, at the Korle-Bu Teaching Hospital in Accra. From what I later learnt, there was no complication. I was born via spontaneous vaginal delivery (SUD).

Interestingly, Eugene was also born in November, but he is a year older than I. When I was old enough to understand the human reproductive system, I assumed that when Eugene was three months old, his dad—our dad—met my mum and they conceived me. If I was born in November, then I was probably conceived in February, so I wondered what kind of man would leave a baby and its mother at home and go to father another child within the same period. From the dossier of negative information I gathered from my mother and the other deductions I made on my own, my perception of Mr. Nelson worsened. My worst recollection of his behaviour was his absence from my naming ceremony.

When I asked my mother why she named me Yvonne, she didn't have any reason. Names have meanings, and parents often choose names to reflect the circumstances surrounding the birth of the child or names that speak to what they expect of their children. Some believe that names have a way of influencing the lives of their bearers so care is often taken to choose names that would not portend doom for the holder. In my case, however, my mother had no reason. I thought Yvonne was an outdated name or what we called "colo" (a Ghanaian colloquialism for "colonial", often used to refer to things that are old-fashioned). But my mother said it was a name that was in vogue in those days.

My own search later revealed that Yvonne has a French origin and is derived from French names such as Yvon, Yves, and Ivo. Yvonne means "yew", a tall and enchanting tree species well-known for its resilience and long life. An entry on thebump.com says the following about that name: "Decorated by delicate green leaves and blood-red wildflowers, yews are one-of-a-kind in every shape and form. With the name Yvonne, a baby can be inspired by nature's beauty each and every day."

Just as I was conceived, my mother may not have been deliberate about my name, but I believe it was the right name for me. I am a yew. I say so not only because I am tall. I believe I still have an awful long way to go, but what has brought me far in life is resilience. It is resilience that kept me in one whole piece after I learnt that I was born by mistake, that I was a product of an aborted plan to abort a pregnancy. It is the resilience of a yew that kept me going when I failed and felt useless to my family and to some friends who did not hide their disdain for the failure I had become.

I believe I am as unique as the yew. And as someone who paints for pleasure, I am often inspired by nature's beauty.

CHAPTER THREE

Meeting Mr. Nelson

When I learnt that Eugene's father also was my father, I began to pay closer attention to him, and a pang of envy started to take a strong hold on me. If we were children of the same father, then I deserved to have what Eugene had—the love and the care and the material possessions. His appearance showed that he was better taken care of than I was. He changed school uniforms more regularly than I did. He had better shoes. Everything of his appeared new all the time. He was dropped off and picked up from school by the man who was also my father, while I had to walk home from school.

My school was about two kilometres from home, and the amount of time needed to cover that distance depended on whether I was going home alone or with my friends. Even with friends, it depended on our number and what occupied our attention after school. Walking was not much of a big deal, but being picked up from school in your father's car came with some prestige, love and care, for which every child yearned.

On a few occasions, my mother drove me to school. Her business kept her occupied most of the time, and considering the distance, I didn't hold any grudge against her for not doing what my father did with Eugene. As a single mother, she had a lot on her plate of hustle, but when she was available and when it was raining, she drove me to school. On some occasions, the father of my friend, Marian Myres, dropped me off in his Volvo before continuing home with his daughter. He was such a nice man, a gesture that made me miss my own father and envy Eugene the more.

What helped me cope with this envy was what my mother told me about Mr. Nelson. When she told me Eugene and I shared the same father, I asked why she hadn't told me all along. Her response was that it was not necessary and would not have changed anything because my father did not really take care of me. He had abandoned me since birth, she said. She gave me a number of scenarios that corroborated her negative portrayal of my father.

Mr. Nelson, she told me, had boycotted my naming ceremony. It was, and still is, a big deal. There must have been something unforgivably grave to cause a man to boycott the naming of his daughter. Whatever the reason was, she did not tell me. And nobody did. But my elder brother thought he had witnessed a fierce fight between my mother and my father shortly after I was born.

32

Enoch was young and could not remember the exact details of the fight, but he said it had something to do with my birth and was so serious that it nearly resulted in fisticuffs. It was on the corridor in our house, he later told me, and they screamed at each other until my father stormed out of the house in anger. That must have been shortly before my naming ceremony. It was not the last of the fights as I later heard from my mother.

My mother told me another story of her visit to my father's shop in Lartebiokoshie when I was still a baby. She had gone there for either provisions or money for my upkeep. When a misunderstanding ensued, she asked my father to take us home if he was not prepared to provide what she requested. My father jumped into his car and drove angrily and carelessly. We almost crashed on our way home, my mother told me.

My mother said when she complained about the dangerous driving, especially when a baby was on board, my father continued to drive like someone on a suicide mission. She then told him to allow us to alight if he wasn't going to drive with care. To her surprise, my father screeched to a halt and ordered us out of his car. She had to find a taxi to take us home.

Hearing these stories did not endear Mr. Nelson to me. I saw him as a total stranger, someone I had no connection with. He must have been the reason my mother wanted to abort me. He would not have abandoned me if he didn't hate me, I told myself. If he loved me,

33

he would have lavished me with gifts and love as he did to Eugene. Beyond the early flood of bad testimonies, what he did when I tried to get close to him confirmed what my mother told me.

On one of our school vacations, I told my mother that I wanted to visit my father and she allowed me to go. Mr. Nelson Okoe was a popular man around Lartebiokoshie in Accra. He was a businessman who loved to have fun. He was the type who threw parties at will and was seen in the company of those who did not subscribe to sacrificing the pleasures of this world for the afterworld. He was successful, and the means to fund that lifestyle was the least of his worries.

That lifestyle came with intended and unintended consequences that transcended his personal behaviour. And it showed when I got to his house. He lived in a big family house, one of the biggest in the area at the time. It was a large family house with two one-storey buildings on the compound. (I remember his twin sister lived in one of the storey buildings.) A number of his children had visited him for the holidays and I was one of them. We were children from different mothers.

I felt different from the rest of the children. They resembled one another and some of them resembled Mr. Nelson. But I looked different. I was tall and the rest were short. The only child taller than me was Eugene's elder brother, Nii Aruna. Nothing showed that the other children and I were of the same father.

I did not feel any bond between Mr. Nelson and me. Nothing drew me to him. There was no fondness. Nothing. If I were to live with this man as my father, then I had to create that bond. I had to psyche myself up and accept that he was my father, despite the things my mother had told me about him. It was going to be difficult, but it was worth a try. Your father, they say, is your father. You can't trade him for someone else's father even if you don't like his looks or character.

I, however, abandoned every effort I was making to create that bond when he clearly told me, without saying it, that I did not belong to his household. It happened in the course of my visit. I was in the living room with the other children when he called all of them to his bedroom. Their laughter and giggling filtered into the living room, where loneliness and neglect were my only companions. I wondered why he did not call me. Eugene was there. He had also been called into my father's room.

When I went home that day, I told my mother that that was my last visit to my father's house. And I kept my word until decades later when circumstances compelled me to go back there. I remember one day, my father was driving past our house and stopped when he saw me sitting at the spot Miranda and I used to sit at. He rolled down and called me, but I refused to go. I remained seated and refused to utter a word, and, after some time, he drove off.

I had asked him for a pair of shoes, and he had promised to buy me three. And that was it. It remained a promise, unfulfilled to date. I was

more emotionally attached to shoes than I was to the man I called my
father. People close to me know that I am infatuated with footwear. I
have about a hundred pairs of them. That love for shoes began very
early, perhaps, as part of the American hip-hop influence. For my
father to deny me shoes meant more to me than he probably could
imagine. It meant he didn't love me. It meant everything my mother
said about him was true.

What hurt me, even more, was the fact that I saw Eugene changing
shoes often. He wore some of the best shoes. It was many years later
that I realised Eugene's wardrobe was supported by his mother, who,
like my mother, was a single mother.

Like me, Eugene was not living with Mr. Nelson. His mother was
different from the mothers of the other children of Mr. Nelson. At
the time, I didn't know this. When I got to know that Eugene, like I,
lived apart from Mr. Nelson, I still wondered why he loved Eugene but
cared less about me. If we were both born out of wedlock, why would
he love one and hate the other? To the best of my knowledge, I had
not offended him. Even if my mother had offended him, why would he
visit her sins on me? And what was the nature of the offence that made
him despise me so much?

It is difficult to miss what you have not tasted, but imagining what I
could have had if there was a father figure in my life gave me a sense of
loss. I was a child starved of parental love. My father was completely
out of the picture, and even though my mother provided for me,

36

I cannot pretend I had a strong bond with the woman who missed no opportunity to remind me that she had me by accident. I don't remember ever doing any homework with my mother. Perhaps, my mother was too busy and my father would have had time for me if I lived under the same roof with him. The worst part of the absence of a father was the improvised father figure at home. My brother Enoch played that role.

It was a role assigned to him by my mother, and I was often at the receiving end of his disciplinarian duties. My elder brother was the man of the house. When I offended my mother and she had to beat me, she sometimes delegated that responsibility to him. It was an assignment he executed with passion, making me wonder whether he beat me so hard just to please my mother or he really wanted to instill discipline in me. He would lock me up in the room and hit me ruthlessly. I remember on one occasion, he beat me and stopped only when I told him I was menstruating. I couldn't tell exactly what he sought to gain, but if it was to make me submissive or subservient to their dictates, then he failed miserably. I was not a pushover. I was strong-willed and didn't let them cheat me at home. I made my position heard and did not allow my background or the rod of discipline and intimidation to force me to accept anything that ran counter to my beliefs, especially when I knew I was right.

All of that made me wonder whether my father would not have treated me differently and whether he would have allowed that to happen to me if he was in the house. Looking at his behaviour at the time, however, I was convinced it could have been worse. We could barely stand each other even though we hardly met. Whatever caused him to invite every one of his children into his room and leave me alone in the hall might have been strong enough to elicit severer beatings from him than what I got from my elder brother. And as I grew, I was determined to find the answer, even if those who had it were unwilling to give it to me.

CHAPTER FOUR

Failed, Dejected and Rejected

My first encounter with what looked like failure was in 2000 when I sat the Basic Education Certificate Examination (BECE), a compulsory transitioning examination administered by the West Africa Examination Council (WAEC). It was the examination that determined who was good enough to enter secondary school. A candidate's performance in that exam also determined whether one was good enough to be admitted into Ghana's "Ivy League" secondary schools. Those who did not excel with distinction were destined for the second class, third class and other unclassifiable secondary schools. Until recently, when the government's policy on protocol admissions and corruption adulterated and still threaten to further undermine the excellence and prestige associated with the elite secondary schools, the dream of every BECE candidate was to make it to the very best secondary schools available. And one way of doing that was to pass extremely well in the BECE.

Candidates were graded using their best six scores in the nine or ten examinable subjects in junior secondary school (Some schools studied and wrote French while others did not so the number of BECE subjects at the time varied from school to school). The scores in a subject were graded from 1 to 9, 1 being the best score or "Excellent", while 9 meant failure in that subject. A candidate's overall score or result was calculated by summing his or her best six scores obtained in the exam. If you were asked what you obtained in the BECE, you said you got an Aggregate 6 or 8, 9 or 10, depending on the total score from your best six subjects.

Those who obtained Aggregate 6 were those who scored 1 in their best six subjects. The exceptional pupils who scored 1 in all the subjects often said, "I got an Aggregate 6 with ten 1's."

The public school system at the basic level has, for a long time, been neglected, so those who go to the public basic schools hardly score Aggregate Six, whether they attend rural or urban public schools. In my days—and that is still the case today—the competition was among those who attended top private basic schools such as St. Martin de Porres School. In such schools, many candidates score "Aggregate Six" so the distinction or comparison is often focused on the number of ones a candidate scores.

This was, perhaps, the reason I felt so distraught when I went for my results and it was a double figure. I obtained Aggregate 12, which meant that I was not among the best. In some public basic schools across the country, that could have been the best score for the exceptionally brilliant children. It could be the best result in some districts, but that was not a good result in St. Martin de Porres. It was the reason I considered myself a failure, especially when that had implications for the secondary school I had to attend.

The outcome of the BECE didn't come to me as a surprise. I was more of an entertainment girl than an academic child. My claim to fame was in music and dance, and I struggled with Mathematics. Social Studies, Religious and Moral Education, and Vocational Skills were the subjects I was good at. English Language was my best. With Integrated Science, I loved only the biology aspect of it. Everything pointed to the fact that I hated figures and calculations. It was the reason I chose General Arts as a course of study in secondary school.

However, it was not always about what I wanted to do. It was what others thought was good for me that prevailed. It is a situation many children face, and mine was no exception. Mine, however, proved costly. I was compelled to study a course I hated in a secondary school I hated even more.

Before we sat our BECE, we were often made to choose the secondary schools we wanted to attend. I don't recall all the three schools I selected for my first, second and third choices, but I remember I wanted to go to Mfantsiman Girls' Secondary School in the Central Region. I don't remember how it was ranked at the time, but that school is currently ranked a Category "A" secondary school in Ghana. Despite my

41

choice, however, I was compelled to attend Aggrey Memorial African Methodist Episcopal Zion Secondary School. I am yet to see a school with a longer name, but what made me hate the school had nothing to do with the length of its name.

Central Region is a citadel of the best secondary schools in Ghana. Being the first capital of the Gold Coast (now Ghana), a number of European missionaries established their schools there and spread to other parts of the country. The Methodist Church established the all-boys Mfantsipim School in 1876. It was the first secondary school in the Gold Coast. Mfantsipim School remains one of the best secondary schools in the country. In terms of the all-girls secondary schools, another educational footprint of the Methodist Church in Cape Coast is the Wesley Girls High School, arguably the most prestigious secondary school in Ghana. The Catholic Church did not want to be outdone so it established St. Agustine's College and Holy Child School, all-boys and all-girls schools respectively. The Anglican Church established the Adisadel College, an all-boys secondary school, and it has also become one of the secondary schools of choice in the country. All of these are category "A" schools in Cape Coast.

The Presbyterian Church and other faiths also made strong marks elsewhere across the country with the establishment of world-class secondary schools, but Cape Coast still remains the town with the largest concentration of the best secondary schools in Ghana. To say you're going to secondary school in Cape Coast came with some prestige. That was, however, not the case with my school.

Aggrey Memorial A.M.E. Zion Secondary School, as we attempted to shorten it, was founded in 1940 by the late Rev. Dr. A. W. E. Appiah. He named the school Aggrey Memorial College after his late uncle, Dr. James Emman Kwegyir Aggrey. Dr. Aggrey was a pan-African intellectual, missionary and educationist who was noted for his advocacy for girl-child education even at a time when the importance of a woman was confined to cooking and childbearing. It was Dr. Aggrey who said, "If you educate a man, you educate an individual, but if you educate a woman, you educate a whole nation."

The secondary school established in his honour, however, started with only boys. According to the official history of the school, "In 1947, the African Methodist Episcopal (A.M.E.) Zion Church took over the realm of affairs of the school as a result of an agreement between the "Aggrey Society" and the A.M.E. Zion Mission. The name of the school was then changed from Aggrey Memorial College to Aggrey Memorial A.M.E. Zion Secondary School, and the first two boarders were also admitted."

It is unclear why the A.M.E. Zion Mission expressed interest in the school, but it may have something to do with the man in whose memory the school was established. In 1898, it was the African Methodist Episcopal Zion Church that gave Kwegyir Aggrey the opportunity to study at Livingstone College, North Carolina, U.S.A., and at the associated Hood Theological Seminary, where he later became a professor.

With student numbers gravitating between 3000 and 4000, Aggrey Memorial—as we further shortened the long name—has been the biggest secondary school in Ghana in terms of population. A school with such numbers and without the corresponding infrastructure and teachers is bound to face challenges. Its victims are those who go there to determine their future.

Things may have improved now, but when I enrolled there in 2000, Aggrey Memorial had no proper supervision and discipline. If you did not pay serious attention to your books, the numbers provided you some form of cover and you enjoyed anonymity from the eyes of the teachers and school authorities whose duty it was to counsel you and put you on the right track. When I realised I was straying too far away from academic excellence, I did not get the needed help and support. Part of the blame ought to be borne by my parents and the school authorities.

In the first place, I did not choose Aggrey. My stepfather, Lt. Col. Davies, had a strong influence in the school. He had been a chairman of either the parent-teacher association or the school's board at some point, so his word carried weight in the school. My two half-siblings had both attended Aggrey Memorial, so when I completed junior secondary school and was made to go there, it was a continuation of a family tradition.

Unlike my siblings, however, I was forced to study a programme against my will. I wanted to study General Arts, but the school said that course was fully subscribed. The only way I could keep my admission was to accept Business Accounting. I hated figures and calculations with passion but I was compelled to pursue that course. In class, all the noise about double entry principles of bookkeeping, balance sheet and the rest of it entered in one ear and went out through the other. I was there to make up the numbers.

My best moments in Aggrey Memorial were on Saturday nights, when we had entertainment. During the week when academic work preoccupied the students, what kept me going was the expectation of Saturday night, when I would mount the stage and perform. I competed in the Miss Aggrey beauty pageant and won, a feat that attracted enmity among the senior girls. A junior girl who won a beauty pageant provided strong competition to the senior girls who aimed to catch the attention of the best boys on offer. There was the assumption that I would be disrespectful because of the crown and attention from senior boys. And it didn't help that I wasn't the quiet and submissive type. I was assertive, which, to the senior girls, was synonymous with arrogance. That was, however, not the main problem I had to contend with in that school.

Aggrey was an experience I didn't prepare for, but it turned out to be a kind of endurance test that prepared me for the future. My mother made sure that my boarding school wooden box (chop box) was always filled with the provisions one needed in a boarding school. She didn't have to buy many of them because she stocked them in her shop and was generous when stocking my box for school. My chop box was what saved me when the dining hall failed me. And it failed me often.

To say that the food was terrible is the mildest way to put the situation in Aggrey Memorial, which defies description. I remember the soup we nicknamed "moftoto". It was either groundnut or palm nut soup. It was so light that if you looked into it, you could see your image. When left untouched for a few minutes, it settled in layers so that the water was on top and the other particles beneath. It was a kind of scientific experiment whose results we didn't make use of. I still grimace at some memories in the dining hall. A friend once saw a toenail in the kenkey he was eating and another student saw the wing of a cockroach in her food. The stories of boarding school food aren't pleasant in many schools, but Aggrey was on a different level.

When our digestive system distilled the nutrients which our teenage bodies needed and we had to discard the rest, it came with another adventure. The toilet and bath facilities were oversubscribed, making it almost impossible to have them in sane and sanitary conditions. Sometimes we bathed outside. And the only way to avoid smelling as if you had swum in the toilet was to resort to what we called "take away".

The girls' dormitory was up the hill. Down beyond it were farms of indigenes of Brafo Yaw, the suburb of Cape Coast where the school is located. "Take away" was simply emptying your bowels in polythene, wrapping it and throwing it as hard as your hands could into the bush. Wherever it settled or how the content spilled was not your business.

If your friend said to you, "I dey go do takeaway," you got the memo.

Not many could stand the harsh conditions of the school. My best friend at the time, Fianko Bossman, told his parents he could not cope and needed a way out. They found a way and he left for Pope John Secondary and Minor Seminary in Koforidua before the second year. Another good friend, Laurina Mensah, left before we got to the third and final year. Her mother came for her to Italy, and that was the last I heard of her.

Those of us without an option had to make two choices, either give up or make the best of the situation. I chose the former. I wasn't an "A" or "B" student. I was just hanging in there, knowing very well that my soul, mind and heart had left the school, but I had to be physically present to tick a box for those who sent me there. Music was what kept me going. It was what helped me to endure, and I couldn't wait to leave the school.

When it was time to leave, the headmaster gave me my worst memory of Aggrey Memorial. The day before my departure from school, he slapped me in a way I would never forget. My offence was that my hair was bushy. We were not allowed to wear our natural hair beyond a certain length. However, the final year girls couldn't wait to have our hair permed or extended, so, in the final term, we preserved it. That was the offence which attracted my worst nightmare in the school.

I left Aggrey resigned to fate. Before WAEC released the results of the 2003 Senior Secondary School Certificate Examination (SSSCE), I knew I could not proceed to the next step on the academic ladder. In that final exam, I did not write Accounting and Costing, two of my four elective subjects. It was a decision I took because it was better to be marked absent than to fail. I didn't know what I was going to write. I could not make meaning of whatever was taught in those subjects.

The dashes I recorded on the SSSCE results sheet did not make any difference from the "Fail" that would have been there had I written the two papers. Either way, I could not go to the university or any tertiary institution without passing at least one of the two subjects I refused to write, especially Accounting. I needed at least three passes in my electives. I barely passed the other two, and my passes in the core subjects were weak.

The future stared at me grimly, blank and bleak. I felt I had wasted my secondary school years. The burden of failure was too heavy to bear. At that point in my life, I had really not figured out what I wanted to do with my life. Education often provided a safe vehicle to escape indecision until much later in life when one decided whether to make a living off one's certificates or confront the world in a different arena of life's many options. If someone wanted to branch into business but did not have the capital, capacity or audacity to abandon school and pursue their dream, they stayed in school. They passed their BECE and SSSCE and went to the university or the polytechnic. They got a degree or diploma or certificate. That was their passport to the next phase of their lives, a licence to work and earn money of their own and live independently until they felt it was time to venture into their true passion.

In my case, the way was not clear. I did not want to do my mother's business or venture into my own. If I had to progress in life, I had to go back to school. I had to face my fears and conquer the two mountains I had avoided at Aggrey. It was either I went back to secondary school and studied a totally different programme that didn't have Accounting and Costing as subjects or I had to resit the two subjects.

Fortunately, WAEC had a private exam mainly for students like me. We called it Nov-Dec because, in those days, it was written in November and December. Here, one was not required to register all the subjects one studied in secondary school. It was an opportunity to resit the subjects one had failed. If a candidate felt the need to improve his or her passes in the other subjects, he or she was free to register for all the subjects. I didn't have the willpower to rewrite all the subjects. I decided to attend private classes and rewrite the two subjects I had avoided.

That experience taught me one of the first most important lessons in life, that difficult situations are better confronted head-on. If you can't negotiate yourself out of it, it is better to fight the haunting giants than postpone the fight, for dodging an inevitable problem or challenge simply means postponing it. If I had averted my mind to this reality early enough, I could have made some modest grades in Aggrey. It would have saved my face. It would have saved me from the dejection and rejection that came with my failure.

I felt rejection at home and from some friends. There was absolutely no respect for me at home. I was a constant irritant, and when I shut the door, it was almost always said to be too loud. I was seen as useless. The fact that my room was full of hip-hop stars was enough confirmation that I was not serious and wouldn't turn out well. I felt like my mother had given up on me at that point. Some friends also distanced themselves from me. Failure is not just an orphan. It can sometimes be an infectious disease, which is avoided by even one's closest associates.

I had a friend called Lerease. She was my closest friend whenever we came back home on secondary school vacation. She was in Wesley Girls and I was in Aggrey, different grades of secondary schools in Cape Coast. But our schools didn't matter when we were back in Dansoman. We partied together and sneaked out to nightclubs together. High school parties, from Adisco to Achimota, did not escape our attention and attendance.

After school, however, the difference in our performance was more distinct than day from night. She gained admission to the University of Ghana and I could not apply to any tertiary institution. I, however, still clung to our friendship. I remember I even went to buy some of her stuff for school from the market. The end of our friendship started with the beginning of her university education. She kept a distance while in school and when she came home on vacation, I noticed a more magnified distance.

Lonely, rejected and almost depressed, I had no option but to give my second attempt at passing my SSSCE all the effort and seriousness I could muster. When the results came, I passed Costing and failed Accounting. If I had to go to school, I needed to pass Accounting. So, in 2005, I had to resit the Accounting paper. It was my "Third World War" and I had already endured enough to know that I could not give up regardless of the outcome of that resit. It was the only way to salvage my self-worth, prove my relevance to my family and prove to friends who shunned my company that I was not a lost cause.

Before I could prove that to them through academic excellence, however, there came an opportunity to be in the limelight. And what I thought had been wasted years in Aggrey Memorial proved to be the most useful experience that would not only prove crucial to me at that point but also define who I would eventually become. It also earned me a place among the "notable alumni" of Aggrey Memorial on the school's Wikipedia page.

One of my first photos

Apart from these photographs, I don't remember what happened in these early years of my life

My mother and my brother propped me up for a photograph on my first birthday.

At manovia with my mum

We took this photo at my mum's shop (manovia)

Spending time at home in our living room in dansoman

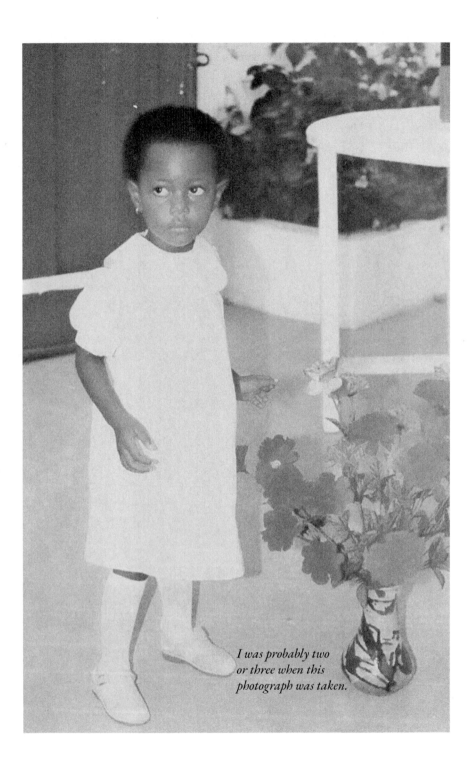

I was probably two or three when this photograph was taken.

My mother, sister and I (being carried) in Dansoman

With my siblings, grandmother and a relative.

From left to right: My brother, my sister and I.

Mr. B.B. Grant, the teacher whose question ignited the search for my father, poses for a photo with me (the tall girl in the middle) and some of my classmates in Class 5A at St. Martin de Porres School.

My primary school days.

Top: *My first year at Aggrey Memorial.*

Bottom: *My final year at Aggrey Memorial*

I [Second from left] was taking it easy with my friends on Aggrey Memorial campus.

With some friends after our BECE in 2000. I'm the one wearing a headband.

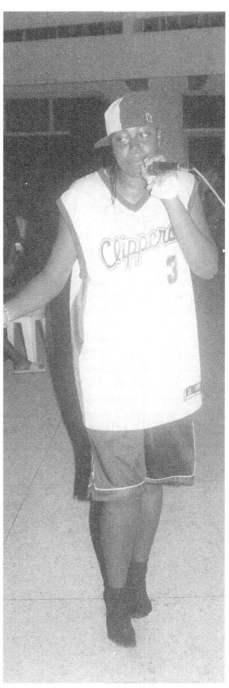

At Aggrey Memorial, I always looked forward to Saturday to mount the stage.

One of my visits to Miranda Mould [in black] in her house

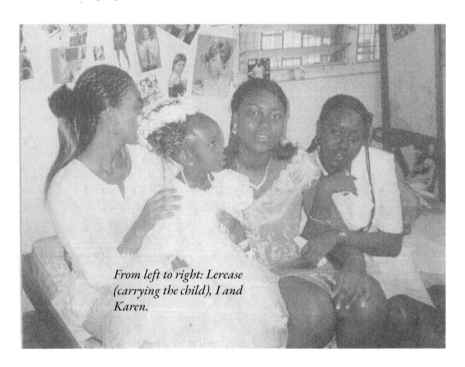

From left to right: Lerease (carrying the child), I and Karen.

With some friends at Central University. Fianko Bossman [second from right] has been one of the most helpful friends in my life.

Karen was that friend through whom some of the best things happened to me.

PART TWO

THE TURNING POINT

CHAPTER FIVE

Abanoma the Miss Ghana Contestant

My mother had remarried by the time I completed secondary school. It was her second attempt at the sacred institution that is said to have been ordained by God. After her divorce from the father of my two siblings, and after having me with Mr. Nelson, she was alone for a long time before she gave marriage another shot. This time, it was with one Mr. Benky, who also lived in Dansoman. When she moved to Mr. Benky's house, she went with me, her youngest child. It was yet another chapter of my life that came with humiliation.

The family of Mr. Benky did not make any attempt to hide their dislike and disdain for my mother and me. It was as if they had sworn to torment us until we were fed up enough to leave the house. When they wanted to whine or say something disparaging about me, something they ordinarily would say out of earshot, they said it in a way that would make me hear it. They would say it in a way that would hurt me.

For instance, they knew my name, but among themselves, they called me "Abanoma." So, instead of "Where is Yvonne?" they would shout, "Where is the Abanoma?"

"What is the meaning of abanoma?" I asked my mother one day.

"It means a stepchild," she explained.

That I was a step-child to Mr. Benky was a fact of life. But did they have to rub it in my face whenever they wanted to say something unpleasant? Well, I could not correct them or stop them from using that name in a way that connoted more illegitimacy than just a way of identifying the person being described. I was used to hearing worse things about me. As harsh as "abanoma" sounded, it was still milder than my own mother reminding me that I was born out of a mistake. As hurtful as it was, it was better than knowing that I was a symbol of regret for the woman who brought me here. It was, however, not the harshest condition I faced in that house.

My room in Mr. Benky's house was truly befitting of an "abanoma". When I first got to the house, the room I was given happened to belong to a daughter of Mr. Benky. She was at the time outside the country. When the real daughter returned, the stepdaughter had to vacate the room.

I was given an adjoining bedroom that shared the same bathroom and toilet with the bedroom of my mother and my stepfather. In order to safeguard their privacy, the opening between the two bedrooms was blocked. Part of the wall of my room on the opposite side was broken to create an outlet to and from my room. That came with its own issues.

To access my room, I had to go through the guest toilet. Part of the wall that was broken to create the new outlet was not plastered. But that was the least of my worries. When Mr. Benky's children decided to watch television in the living room for hours, water from the leaking air conditioner dripped into my room so I had to keep an eye on the container that was used to collect the water from the air conditioner. On occasions that I went out and the air conditioner functioned the whole day, I returned to a room flooded with water. Apart from this ordeal, I didn't have a bathroom of my own, after being blocked out of the shared bathroom and toilet meant for the room I occupied. I used the guest toilet, but when I had to bathe, I did it behind my room, near the dogs' kennel.

This meant I didn't have the freedom to bathe at any time of the day. I did so under the cover of darkness and I had to first ensure that there wasn't anybody peeping into the compound before I undressed and took my bath. I was hitting 20 and my feminine features were ripe and in their prime. It was the time I was most sensitive to my body and valued my privacy the most, but being in a hostile terrain, I had to cope with what I had and forget about what I needed or deserved. My female friends who visited and had to bathe also went through this adventure.

When I could no longer bear it, I asked my mother to let me go back to our house. She agreed, but I wasn't going back to the comfort I had vacated. My mother had rented the main building out, and my sister, who had married, lived in the boys' quarters with her family. My brother lived in the extension upstairs and the only space left at the time was a tiny room in the middle, which did not have a toilet or bath. I remember Irene Logan, the Ghana-based Liberian singer who won the 2006 Stars of the Future reality show, once visited me and when I told her my room had no toilet and bath, she was surprised. Having to go outside the room into the compound to access a toilet and a bath was uncomfortable, especially late in the night or when it rained, but it was normal to me. The only abnormality was that I was no longer a normal girl struggling to pass her exam and enter the university. I was on my way to stardom. It began with a beauty pageant.

Some of the best things that have happened to me came through an angel with whom God blessed me as a friend. Karen Okata Boateng is one of those friends who stick tighter and love deeper than family. We both attended secondary school in Cape Coast, but that was not the reason we were friends. I was closer to Lerease than Karen because Lerease and I lived a few blocks apart. However, in my moment of failure, Karen did not make me feel inadequate. She is the type of friend who believes in you more than you believe in yourself.

It was Karen who first mooted the idea of me contesting the Miss Ghana beauty pageant. It was in 2005, and I was yet to go to the university. Those were the days when the pageant carried a lot of prestige and was highly coveted and I didn't see myself anywhere near the crown.

"You're tall, intelligent and beautiful. Why don't you go for Miss Ghana?" I remember Karen telling me.

It sounded good to be told this, but my immediate response was self-doubt. The contestants were often university graduates or students of tertiary institutions, but I was neither a graduate nor a student in any tertiary institution. Karen was relentless. She said she knew someone who could guide and advise me if I agreed to take part. That person was Stacy Amoateng of TV3's Music Music fame. The audition had started, and when we eventually approached the organisers, they said we had to go through the process.

Their main concern was my weight, but I promised to work on it. It wasn't just a promise I made to persuade them. I was determined to do that. With the help of Karen, we went to Dansoman Roundabout and bought four-inch high-heeled shoes. While I was dieting and exercising to shed some weight, I was also learning to walk like a model. It wasn't an easy task for a girl who was a tomboy, but there was the will. And, with the help of Karen, I found a way.

In 2005, Shirley Frimpong Manso's Sparrow Productions was the franchise holder of the Miss Ghana pageant. Our base was the office of Sparrow Productions. The competition was keen. When you have 10 young women fighting for a crown, fighting to catch the attention and win the favour of organisers, fighting to impress the judges of the competition and the voting Ghanaian public; the good, the bad, and the ugly side of the competition could not be exaggerated. The

68

organisers seemed to have their favourites, and I believed I wasn't anybody's favourite. However, I won the favour of the audience.

On the Saturday before the grand finale, I was featured on the front page of *The Spectator* newspaper, one of the top weekend publications at the time. Many in the competition thought I was influential enough to get it done for me or that I paid for it. If anybody paid money on my behalf, I did not know. I had no such influence or cash to sponsor a front-page publication. I felt I was just lucky and had favour where it mattered. It was also, perhaps, because I was tipped to win the contest and those who wanted to sell their papers obviously wanted to associate with the best, the potential winner.

A Ghana News Agency report on the grand finale of the 2005 Miss Ghana competition, which is still online, said the following of the expected outcome of the contest that night: "The contest was a straight fight between Lamisi Mbilla and Yvonne Nelson, who also won the most talented and photogenic lady and took home 2 million [today's 200] cedis."

It is true that I won two individual awards on the night and was tipped to be crowned Miss Ghana. Before the final announcement, however, I knew my fate. I knew I would not wear the crown. The miracle I hoped would happen did not. So, I was not surprised I missed out. I had fumbled when it was my turn to answer the question that was asked the final five contestants from whom the first three winners would be picked.

I remember, backstage, Shirley Frimpong Manso came to hold me tenderly and asked, "Yvonne, why?"

She and I didn't have a close relationship, but I imagined she was rooting for me to win. That slip obviously took me out of the frontrunners at that point of the race. It was the wish of many that I would emerge with the crown, but it did not happen. I didn't make the headlines.

Lamisi Mbillah of the University of Ghana made headlines as Miss Ghana 2005. The first runner-up was also a University of Ghana student, Ursula Naa Dei Neequaye, while Maame Afua Anne Darko of the University of Cape Coast was adjudged the second runner-up.

I entered the competition because I wanted to win. To lose the crown, especially in the manner in which it happened, was painful. Seeing that the first three winners were all university students and I was a secondary school leaver who had not qualified to enter the university increased the intensity of my desire to excel academically, even if my version of excellence, in my wildest imagination, was just the opportunity to gain admission into a university.

Looking back, however, I do not regret not winning the beauty pageant. The odds that I would not have been here if I had won that contest are very high. I would have spent eternity basking in the glory and opportunities that came with the crown. My life would have been defined by the rules governing the competition. I don't know whether I would have survived the trappings of the fame that came with being

Miss Ghana. I know I would have ceased to be an ordinary girl. The restricting power of living according to other people's expectations of Miss Ghana may have prevented me from being who I wanted to be. It could have stopped me from doing what I wanted to do.

The Miss Ghana pageant, however, gave me some exposure that would later serve as a launchpad to something greater. At the time I lost the crown, I had no bragging rights to anything I was proud of. The benefit I had derived from my education until that stage of my life was entertainment. The singing, dancing and mounting of the stage at St. Martin de Porres and Aggrey Memorial came in handy during the Miss Ghana contest. I was adjudged the most talented contestant because I had spent much of my life singing and dancing. I wrote the rap songs I performed in that competition.

My fumbling at the intellectual test was what cost me a crown, and I vowed not to let anything come between me and my education should I pass the Nov-Dec. While I was pushing and fighting for my own way, Providence seemed to have the final say. A golden opportunity, out of nowhere, jolted me pleasantly.

CHAPTER SIX

Princess Tyra

It is said that the big game often appears when the hunter has given up the hunt for the day. I cannot say I had completely given up on life's hunting, but it was a thought that creeped in and out of my mind as I confronted my world. My life at that moment was dogged by what I thought were crushing failures and disappointments. Crashing out of Miss Ghana when the crown was in sight and well within my reach was the defeating icing on my cake of struggle and self-doubt. If I couldn't do well in school, and my only attempt at a competition in the entertainment industry did not work, where else could I make it?

I would later learn that it was only a matter of time. When that time was ripe, I didn't have to struggle or fight for the tight window of opportunity that allowed the glowing rays of hope into my life once again. It happened as though I was cast in a movie whose perfect script was written and directed by Providence, and I was merely a favoured cast. In reality, that's how I entered the movie industry—effortlessly.

It was in 2006, and I was with Karen Okata, the bearer of my luck charm. Even when she didn't have to play an active role, Karen was always connected in some way to the monumental epochs of my life. It so happened that she was with me when I bumped into what would turn out to be the golden door that opened priceless opportunities for me.

We had gone to Afrikiko, a middle-class eatery and recreational centre in Accra, to buy fried rice. A friend I had met in my Miss Ghana days and I were in the car while Karen went into the restaurant to get us the food, which we intended to take away. When Karen kept too long, my hunger pangs nudged me to follow up to see what was holding her up. It was on my way to the restaurant that I bumped into Abdul Salam Mumuni, a renowned movie producer in Ghana. When he mentioned his name, I instantly recognised him, for he was a household name in the entertainment industry and I had watched a number of movies from his Venus Productions. I am not sure whether he also made me out, but, having taken part in Miss Ghana and come close to winning, he probably knew who I was.

"Are you coming for the audition?" he asked me after the introduction.

I had no idea he was auditioning for his next movie, and I told him just that. I was there for food and nothing was going to distract me. Even when he invited me to join in the audition, I didn't have any difficulty choosing food over a potential movie role that day. That was how the brief encounter ended—without any interest or commitment from my side. In the entertainment industry, music was my first love. I had acted in school, but at the time I met Abdul Salam, as he's popularly known, I wasn't excited about the prospects of being on the screen, especially when my first two attempts had ended in smoke.

After Miss Ghana, I had been cast in a television series titled *Babe Town*. It was a series produced by actress and producer Luckie Lawson, and the entire episode was shot in a barber's shop. It never made it onto television.

Before *Babe Town*, Ivan Quashigah, the producer of *Things We Do for Love*, featured me in another television series titled *Fortune Island*. In that series, I played a detective. I was going to crime scenes, examining dead bodies and all that. I don't remember much about the storyline now. At the time I met Abdul Salam, that series too had not yet made it to any screen, so jumping at an impromptu invitation to audition for a movie role was not a particularly exciting prospect. It was part of the reason I didn't regret choosing food over an audition, but I did leave my contact details.

That destiny-shaping encounter did not, however, end with my rejection of the invitation to audition. Abdul Salam called later and offered me a role in the movie. I had just started my first year at Central University College (CUC). I had managed to pass my Accounting and Costing after two attempts and applied to CUC to study Human Resource Management. If you asked me why I chose that programme of study, I would struggle for a reason. What I studied at the time was inconsequential to me. What mattered was that I was in the university. I had bought the form and applied quietly. My mother and siblings only got to know about my plans when I was offered admission. It was my moment of pride and the pleasant surprise was acknowledged by my family.

Having suffered rejection and humiliation from some of my friends because of my inability to go to the university after secondary school, I had vowed that nothing would stand between me and the degree I desperately needed. I had learned from my basic and secondary education that I was good enough to pass examinations, but my main obstacles were self-imposed obstructions. If I would graduate with a degree after four years, then it all depended on me. CUC is a private university and is more expensive than a public university. At the time, the fees at CUC were about four times what my mates paid at public universities in Ghana. I could not afford to waste my mother's colossal investment and leave after four years with nothing to show.

This was what made it difficult to accept Abdul Salam's offer of a movie role. After some persuasion, however, I gave it a try, but with a grim determination not to let that derail my academic journey.

The first movie I featured in was Beyonce. It had Nadia Buari as the lead actor and I played a role that my Nigerian colleagues in the movie industry call a *decorated walker pass*. I was merely decorated to walk past, without anything notable in my appearance. I was the lead actor's friend and I played only one scene that had lines. Various reviews of the movie online do not have my name as part of the cast, and that is perfectly understandable. I was almost anonymous.

My breakthrough didn't take long to come. It came with an urgent call, again, from Abdul Salam. I was in the lecture hall and stepped out to answer the call. He needed me for a movie role. The crew and cast were already on location and I had to come straight away, he said on the phone.

When I got there, my costumes were ready. I was dressed like a princess and asked to go on set. The conventional processes of being given a script, mastering it and attending script conferences or rehearsals were all side-stepped. It appeared someone had been given that role but had to be replaced. An improvised cast was expected to take her place, so the lots fell on me. With verbal instruction on who I was and what I was expected to do, I was thrust onto the set, like a fat goat being thrown into a den of ravenous hyenas. That was how I felt when the unmasked disapproval of my inclusion was communicated in the most unvarnished of languages. I fumbled on set. I felt uncomfortable in the costume. I had no time to psychologically prepare myself for the role. But here I was acting in a movie that had my character as the title. The movie was *Princes Tyra*.

And I was Princess Tyra.

In that movie, Kofi Adjorlolo was my father, the king. He got so frustrated with my acting that he walked off the set in protest and told Abdul Salam to replace me. (A few years later, I cast Kofi Adjorlolo in a movie I produced). The director, Frank Raja Arase, did not have any hope in me either. I felt terrible, lost confidence and became anxious.

Princess Tyra had a number of maids. I confided in one of them that that day was going to be the last time they would see me. I had endured enough embarrassment and was not going to show up again. What I said got into the ears of Abdul Salam Mumuni, and he spent a considerable amount of time convincing me not to abandon the project. It appeared he was the only one in the production team who had confidence in my ability to act. Rooting for me sparked wild rumours that he had something to do with me, the only possible reason he wanted me around despite my abysmal performance.

I later learnt that the line between that perception and the reality in the movie industry was imperceptible. It is true that most movie producers in the industry take advantage of women who need opportunities. It is almost a norm that you cannot break through with just your talent. If you are a woman, you have to give something to get something. If a male producer was resisting all pressures to dismiss a young woman, the only possible reason among those present, therefore, was that the two were involved in something beyond the movie.

The movie industry is one of the most hostile environments for young and budding talents. There isn't much encouragement from senior colleagues, especially among women. A new entrant is often seen as a competitor who is there to take someone's shine or snatch a role meant for them. The default position of the old guns is hostility and a silent prayer for the novice to fail. There are, however, a few with exceptionally kind hearts. One such person is Jackie Appiah.

Jackie Appiah was one of my maids in *Princess Tyra*. She was the maid Van Vicker, my lover prince from another kingdom, fell in love with. Jackie had made quite a name for herself in the industry even before I entered, but she didn't at any point make me feel less of myself. She treated me well and gave me all the encouragement. Apart from the convincing Abdul Salam did when he learned of my intention to abandon the production, Jackie made my stay less of a burden. Of hostilities on set, I must say I also felt very comfortable whenever I was on set with Majid Michel.

I had a change of mind after the encouragement from the producer so I decided to give *Princess Tyra* my level best. I summoned courage, gathered confidence and faced my fears. If people think you're not good enough, the most appropriate response is to show, rather than tell them what you can do. Instead of abandoning the movie, I stayed and fought on. And the rest, as they say, is history.

The opening of *Princess Tyra* lists the stars as Van Vicker, Jackie Appiah, Kofi Adjorlolo, Kalsoume Sinare, Rama Brew, Gavivina Tamakloe and:
"Introducing Yvonne Nelson."

Princess Tyra was well-received, and it is still one of my biggest movies of all time. It was big in the fame and opportunities it gave me. I earned 1.5 million cedis from that movie. Today (in November 2022) that is 150 cedis or $11. At the time, however, it was worth about $100.

That was half of the amount I earned for participating in Miss Ghana. I had saved the entire amount I earned from Miss Ghana. I also saved the entire money I earned for playing the lead role in *Princess Tyra*. Looking back, the financial reward was peanuts, but the exposure that the movie gave me was priceless.

I became a household name. My mother could not hide her pride when a church member at Mount Olivet Methodist Church in Dansoman approached her after church one Sunday and all she had to tell my mother was how well I acted in that "popular movie". Prior to that, I had been a nuisance that was barely tolerated whenever I returned from set late and woke them up to open the gate for me. I remember my mother once remarked that I always said I was acting, but there was nothing to show for it.

The release of *Princess Tyra* changed everything. My status at home changed. My brother and sister now saw me as a celebrity sister. The posters of celebrities that littered the walls of my room were still there, but the disdain that had accompanied them vanished overnight. There was respect for my name at home and my sister even added "please" to the words she spoke to me.

The recognition went beyond my family. I attracted more movie roles from other producers and I started starring in movies that had me as the main character or the only big-name character driving the movie. The movies I featured in after *Princess Tyra* are *Passion and Soul*, *The Prince's Bride*, *Material Girl*, *Playboy*, *Heart of Men*, *The Game*, and *4play Reloaded*, among others.

I did not, however, have a smooth sail. The fame and its trappings, the opportunities and the rewards and my journey to the top were rudely interrupted. It came from the least expected source, where my breakthrough began.

CHAPTER SEVEN

Banned by Movie Producers

The way to the top is not always a leisurely and pleasurable walk in the park. It is not a tarred road bedecked with roses. It is a rough and thorny path. It can sometimes be slippery too. The journey through this path requires perseverance and endurance if one is to see brightness beyond the dark and gloomy clouds of natural and man-made obstacles. I learned this the first day I went on set to shoot *Princess Tyra*. But what appeared later made my experience at the beginning of the *Princess Tyra* movie pale into insignificance. The obstacles came in different forms—physical and spiritual.

The first notable spiritual attack happened when I was shooting *Material Girl*. A lady who worked with Abdul Salam reminded me that it was the first movie I was leading, without any other big-name or established actors. She said if the movie didn't go well, the producer would not cast me again. I don't know why she said that, but I took it as a cautionary piece of advice that should spur me on to put in my level best. I was determined to do that, but the obstacles were beyond my control.

When we started shooting, I had a problem with my eye. It reddened and was painful. When I visited the hospital, the doctor said it was a bacterial infection or something to that effect. I was given medication, but it only got worse. Part of the reason I wore sunglasses in that movie was to conceal the reddened eye. I could mask the pain with smiles and act as though everything was normal, but the cameras could not do anything about a defective eye of the lead actor.

When it worsened and we could not continue to shoot, especially with some indoor scenes, we had to put the production on hold until I healed. If there was any change in my condition as we waited, it was only getting worse. It both frustrated and scared me. I could feel the tension around me when I was offered that challenge at a very young age in my acting career. It made me feel there could be something more to my condition than just a physical irritation of that part of my body.

I locked myself up in the room for a whole day, stripped naked, lay on the floor and prayed and cried to God. I wasn't someone who could be described as very spiritual, but I had seen the hand of God in my life many times and knew He could intervene in this crucial stage of life He had placed me. It was a crazy act of faith, but it worked. The following day, my eye cleared. And two days later, I was on set. *Material Girl* was a huge success, and it did not erase my favour in the eyes of Abdul Salam and other producers as the woman had warned. It opened more opportunities that came with their own hostilities.

The most hostile obstacle I faced at the time was not spiritual. Even if it was, it manifested in a physical form with known human causal agents. It happened in 2010 when the Film Producers Association of Ghana, a bunch of men whose behaviour I found to be disgraceful, decided to ban me from acting for one year.

It all started with my altercation with Abdul Salam Mumuni, the man who gave me my breakthrough. The misunderstanding between us did not warrant a ban. I saw it more as someone who felt entitled to me and wanted to show me where power lay. It was no doubt that he gave me the opportunity to shine when no one else believed in me. I was, and still am, eternally grateful to Abdul Salam. But what I could not do was lose my voice to fight for my right because he had helped me. I had always stood up for myself and others in situations of injustice and didn't think I should not complain about unfair treatment just because he had helped me.

My fight with Abdul Salam—if I can call it a fight—happened when we were acting *4Play Reloaded*. I was in my final year at Central University when Abul Salam called me to join the cast. He was well aware of my commitment to academic responsibilities and that I didn't have much time to spare. I was not ready to defer my programme, and leaving CUC without a degree would leave me in despair. But he still acted in a way that was totally unfair.

I had sacrificed a quiz and answered an urgent call to go on set for the shoot when he called me. I left campus and went to sit the whole day, but there was no show. One of the lead characters did not show up. The following day, I again abandoned class and went for the shoot, but nothing happened. One of the lead actors, we were told, was a judge in the Miss Malaika beauty pageant. Those responsibilities had kept her away and kept me at bay from academic work.

When I was leaving that day, I told Abdul Salam that I had already missed two days of class and a quiz, so I wasn't coming the following day. What I said was as if I had struck a match stick and dropped it in fuel. He flared up and started a condescending attack on me. I have never seen him angrier. Roger Quartey, one of the crew members, kept fueling his ego and stoking the fire that raged until I left that day.

I didn't receive any call to go back on set for the shoot. The next time I heard from or about him was a week later when I heard in the media that FIPAG had banned me from acting for a year. It was the top story on every entertainment show. Social media and newspapers used it as the cud they ruminated on from time to time. When I had an opportunity, I told my side of the story, but the popular narrative was that I was a young "disrespectful and ungrateful actress fighting those who had made her who she is".

I must admit it was a tough year. I was in my final year at the university. I was banned from acting. I was pregnant and definitely was not prepared to host another human being.

I also felt betrayed by my colleagues in the movie industry, especially the older female actors. I thought I was being bullied and needed their support to confront the all-male producers. If what they did to me was to send a message to those they employed to act for them; if that message was to say that nobody was indispensable and that they could choose to teach anyone they pleased a lesson; then I expected a collective voice of disapproval from the actors. That did not happen. I was alone. And I faced it squarely.

Here again, one exception was Majid Michel, who stood by me in the thick of it all. He defended me and even tried to mediate with Abdul Salam, but it did not work. He was one of three people with whom I travelled to Akosombo to see the film producers, who had said they wanted to meet me. The others were Fred Nuamah and Frank Raja.

In Akosombo, I saw Augustine Abbey, popularly known as Idikoko, among the film producers. This was a man I grew up watching on television and hoped he would encourage and inspire the young ones to grow. Instead, he was siding with a group of men who thought they controlled the bread and the whip and had the power to deny a bite to whoever refused to be whipped in their incongruous line. In the meeting, they were extremely rude.

I still do not understand why they wanted to meet me, for nothing concrete came out of that meeting. Perhaps, they thought I would go and kneel and beg them to lift my ban. I didn't do that. Frank Raja, Majid and I left Akosombo without any sign from them that they would do something about the ban. It continued.

Within that year, however, there were cracks in the ranks of the producers. David Owusu of Media Five Productions defied the ban and cast me in a movie, but he was not allowed to release it until the ban was over.

Abdul Salam, who had instigated the ban came to me to patch things up. He said we should leave the past behind us and work together. With him, I shot two movies. This was without the knowledge of the other producers because the ban was still in place. Socrates Sarfo, a producer who asked me out for dinner, told me how he was disappointed in the actions of Abdul Salam.

I don't know why they all suddenly disembarked from their high horses and tried to court my affection. If I'm to hazard a guess, however, I'll pin it down to the failure of the intended effect of their ban. They had thought I was going to be crushed by the ban, but they soon realised that their action had rather lifted my profile.

My name was on the lips of many. Those who hadn't paid attention to me were beginning to find out more about me. While I launched my glaucoma foundation and tried to give back to society in my own small way, a floodgate of opportunities opened in Nigeria for me and I featured in a number of Nollywood movies. Their intended lull in my career turned out not to be the dull moment they had anticipated. Acting in Nigeria was more lucrative than in Ghana. There were times I shot multiple movies on a single Nigerian trip before I returned to Ghana. If Ghana gave me a professional breakthrough in acting, my financial breakthrough came from acting in Nigeria. This is a fact many Ghanaian actors who have featured in Nigerian movies will not dare contest. Nigeria has a bigger market and an even bigger budget for movies.

So, before I became active again in Ghana, I had also become very popular with some of the top producers in Nigeria. If the Ghanaian producers thought they were putting an unbearable weight on my head to break me, they ended up strengthening my neck and preparing me for heavier and more rewarding burdens of life.

CHAPTER EIGHT

Abortion

It was 2010. And I was 25. I was about to graduate with a degree. My acting career had taken off extremely well, but it was hit with a ban in Ghana. I found a welcome distraction in my charity, the Yvonne Nelson Glaucoma Foundation. I recorded a single that featured some of the top stars in the entertainment and sports industries in Ghana. Musicians such as Sarkodie, Efya, Sherifa Gunu and Edem were featured. Michel Majid, boxer Joshua Clottey, Nana Aba Anamoah, Prince David Osei and John Dumelo also featured in the video.

The solace I sought in my humanitarian venture and opportunities in Nigeria was interrupted by a turmoil that started mildly in my abdomen and climbed wildly to my head and gave me sleepless nights. In my head was not physical pain. It was mental torture.

I had gone for a pregnancy test to confirm what becomes the most obvious conclusion for a sexually active young woman who misses her monthly flow. I was in the company of Karen. And when the test result was ready, I wasn't strong enough to open it. She did and declared the verdict.

"Charlie, it dey there!" she exclaimed.

On an ordinary day, I would have laughed out loud and that would trigger a string of jolly conversations and jokes. But this was no laughing matter. It was a grim piece of information that was capable of turning my world upside down. I wasn't the only one responsible for the situation, so I called the man whose potent seed had germinated in me. His name is Michael Owusu Addo, a renowned Ghanaian musician who is better known as Sarkodie.

Sarkodie was a budding musician with the potential to become one of the biggest artists in Ghana and beyond. At the time, however, the future looked uncertain, and his way through the maze of life still appeared too foggy to predict. Success was not guaranteed. He was still living with his mother and was not ready to carry a burden while he was being carried by his mother.

I wouldn't call what had developed between us a serious relationship. I gravitated toward people in the music industry. For the longest time in my life, music was my getaway from all the unpleasant things life threw at me. So, I liked his talent. We started talking and got close. Closer.

And extremely close. Then the unexpected happened.

I was 25, and he was 22. I won't say I was too young to know how to protect myself, but I think I was naïve. I was still that tomboy transitioning to womanhood and knew very little about the most important things about women. I knew nothing about safe periods and ovulation and the complexities of the monthly. I grew up with my mother but "vagina" and "penis" were like taboo words in our house. The closest she had come to giving me sex education was when she once forcibly opened my legs to inspect my hymen. After that, she warned me that if I broke my virginity, she would grind pepper and ginger and insert it down there.

That was in my teen years. I was now much older and more independent, but I still knew next to nothing about my reproductive system and its cycle. I knew, at that age, that I could get pregnant. I tried to abstain as much as possible, and when it had to happen, I protected myself. But I lost my guard with Sarkodie and had to pay dearly.

I called him on the phone and said we needed to talk. He still lived with his mother and this was not the kind of news to break in the house. I called him out of the house when I got to Tema, and we sat in my Toyota Rav4. (He drove a Toyota Matrix at the time if my memory serves me right).

I sensed the intensity of his emotions when I broke the news to him. I could hear his heart pounding, and when he finally found his voice, he faltered. His message was, however, unambiguous. He didn't want the pregnancy. That would damage him and his career. The only option was to get rid of it.

Whether or not his career and the uncertainty of life were the real reasons he could not afford to let me keep the pregnancy, I cannot tell. I later discovered that he had a girlfriend who was attending a university outside the country. It was in her absence that he got involved with me and things got dangerously complicated. Whatever it was, his stance was clear. And I was left to evaluate my own options.

The first thing that hit me when he said no to keeping the pregnancy was my own life. I had grown up without a father in my life. I had often been reminded of how I had been borne by mistake. I was still wondering if the man whose name I bore was my father. How was I going to bring another human being into this world to live like me, someone whose father would reject him or her as Mr. Nelson had rejected me? If there was a way to spare someone else the trauma I was contending with, why would I reject that option, especially when I was not psychologically and emotionally prepared to be a mother?

In my circles, only two of my friends knew about my pregnancy. If someone else knew apart from the three of us, I don't know who told that person. I later discovered that Sarkodie's team also knew about it.

As I wondered what to do next, a friend of mine said she knew of a certain pill that I could take and get rid of the foetus before it festered.

She was in a hostel and had a room to herself. That made her hostel the ideal place to do it. If I tried it at home, my mother would know about it. And hell would come crashing down on an already troubled earth.

So, one weekend, I visited her and took the pills. I swallowed one and inserted the other into my vagina. The few days that followed were some of the most excruciatingly painful moments of my life. It was only after I gave birth that I was able to get a condition to liken the pain I felt to. The pain came with severe bleeding that lasted so long that I became weak. I could see life slipping out of my frail body. When I sat on the WC, clots of blood fell into the toilet bowl like constipated poop. When the bleeding and pains finally stopped, I went to do another pregnancy test to ascertain the efficacy of the self-administered procedure.

The pregnancy was still there, intact.

Keeping the pregnancy was not an option. Undertaking another self-medication was also not an option. I agreed with Sarkodie that, this time, we had to do it in a hospital or health facility. Again, that friend of mine had a recommendation. It was a facility in Mamprobi, and, on the appointed day, Sarkodie drove me there with his manager and they left.

Having endured the life-threatening but failed attempt, the question I asked myself while entering the facility was, *Is this where my life will end?* The dilapidation of the building that housed the doctor's operation did not inspire any hope in me that it would be safe. I was given an injection that was supposed to numb the pain, but I could still feel it. I could feel the screwing inside me. I even thought my entire womb was being removed. Whatever it was, my only prayer was for a successful outcome.

From the health facility, I went back to my friend's hostel. As had happened with my Nov-Dec exams after school, I hoped and prayed that I would be lucky with this second attempt. The pain, again, was intense and I bled profusely. I felt worse because Sarkodie left me to my fate in the most difficult period. He did not call to check up on me or find out how the procedure had gone.

Having an abortion is one of the most regrettable mistakes in my life. If the clock of life could be rewound to my younger self, I would keep it. But the benefit of hindsight is sometimes not useful because the lessons learned cannot be applied retrospectively.

I don't know how others who have been through it feel, but my abortion haunted me for years. For instance, whenever I visited the gynaecologist and had to fill out a form, there was a place on the form that asked whether I had had an abortion before. Knowing that it was important to be truthful in my disclosure to health professionals, I had to tick the abortion box. It was not just a tick, but the disclosure of my moment of shame in a judgmental society, sharing a dreaded piece of secret with people whose perception of me might never be the same.

I have encountered many young women who have gone through this with varied stories of pain and degrees of regret. I have also heard stories about others whose situations and reasons for going the painful and dangerous route were not different from mine. Some have not been as lucky as I have. They either lost their lives or their ability to have children again. Like me, they are often pushed by the financial burden of mothering a child alone, the emotional and psychological unpreparedness or the unwillingness of our society to accept children born out of wedlock. Apart from everything else, my mother, a prominent member of the Methodist Church, would have ostracised me had she known about my pregnancy at the time. Looking back, however, I still believe I acted foolishly. I could have lost my life. My body could have been imperiled with an irreversible condition that would have left me damaged forever.

The fear of the unknown can be paralysing, but in an attempt to mitigate it, it is sometimes difficult to notice the seriousness of the situations we sometimes put ourselves into. If I had taken the risk of delivering, I might have pulled through despite the difficulties. It is almost always impossible to change a situation that becomes clearer many years later. In some cases, however, the lessons learned from the past become useful blueprints for present and future decisions. Some do not get second chances, but I was lucky I did. When I became pregnant the second time, I didn't think twice about keeping it.

This time, I was mature enough to know that what mattered most was how my child and I fared. My preoccupation was the kind of future

I would help the child build and thrive in. What others thought and what society said about my unconventional way of procreation became secondary. The tongues that wagged about the inappropriateness of having a baby without first having a husband did not move me this time. I was mature enough not to pay heed to those whose next question after learning of Yvonne Nelson's pregnancy would be, "Who is her husband?"

I was financially stable enough to fend for a child and give it a bright start to life. With that in mind, I was a hundred percent sure about the decision I took to keep my second pregnancy.

And I did not need to consult anybody about it. I did not need any validation of that decision from any man or woman, young or old.

CHAPTER NINE

First Car, First House and Independence

I started to appreciate and yearn for space after I returned from my sojourn in Mr. Benky's house. Before my mother's marriage to Mr. Benky fell on the rocks, I had had enough of the humiliation there so I left before my mother followed. My first taste of an independent adult life began when I returned to my mother's house. That was when I took part in the Miss Ghana contest, started acting and was in the university. At that stage of my life, I was responsible for myself, pushing through my fledgling acting career while studying to acquire a degree.

One of my first tangible assets was a rice cooker I bought during that period. That piece of life-saving equipment ensured that I had enough to eat and didn't have to go out on an empty stomach. It also helped me to save because it cut down my budget for food considerably. I have grown to have an emotional attachment to rice cookers because of the first one I bought. If a rice cooker was the first tangible asset I acquired, the first and most expensive property I acquired was a car.

My first car was a used Toyota Corolla. In Ghana, that is the template almost everyone follows. Very few people are able to buy brand-new cars as beginners. But the joy in owning a used car—if that is your first—is indescribable. In my case, it did not matter that it was a used car. I bought it from De-Georgia Motors in Tesano, Accra. It was the biggest status symbol that magnified my name at home and put some modicum of respect on my brand at the time. My elder brother drove an old VW Jetta while my mother drove a Nissan Sentra. At the time my Toyota Corolla arrived, it was the nicest car in our house, and I worshipped it. I washed it myself.

I don't remember how much it cost, but it wasn't very expensive. I could, however, not pay in full so I paid half and the rest was spread over six months. Abdul Salam had promised me roles in a couple of movies in the period so I worked hard so that I did not have to default in paying for my most valuable asset. It solved a number of problems. This was in 2007 or thereabouts when there were no cab-hailing applications. What this meant was that whenever I needed a taxi, I had to walk to the roadside or a vantage point where I could get one. The inconvenience, especially at night or on rainy days, made owning a car a necessity, not a luxury.

My life at the time was a personification of hustling and the car was an integral part of that important chapter of my drive to succeed. I used to carry my costumes to school and would dash to shoot movies after lectures. That vehicle served a dual purpose as a means of transport and a private office that housed my clothes, shoes, make-up kits and everything else I needed at work.

Two years later, I bought my second car, a golden-brown Toyota Rav4. It was also a used vehicle but it was in better shape than the Corolla, which had started to break down and give me problems. I had got a car dealer to take the Corolla and I paid a top-up to acquire the Rav4.

After three years, the RAV4 also began to give me problems. Besides the mechanical issues I had to grapple with, my brand was growing, and in the showbiz industry, an actress who had courted enormous media and national attention for the right and wrong reasons didn't have to show up at functions in a rickety vehicle. So, for the first time, I bought a brand-new vehicle or what they call here "tear rubber".

It was a VW Touareg, which I ordered in 2010 and was delivered in 2011. It made a lot of waves in my circles and I was immensely proud of myself. In 2019, I bought a BMW saloon car, which I still use together with the 2011 Touareg. With time, I outgrew the glitzy lifestyle of the industry. If changing a vehicle every other year is part of the show business, then I prefer something worthier and more impactful to show than a fleet of vehicles. At the time, however, investing in the optics was more worthwhile than in the substance.

The showbiz industry comes with demands and expectations, some of which are impossible to meet. I was fortunate to have been shaped by the circumstances surrounding my birth. The early taste of failure and its concomitant rejection taught me to set my priorities right when luck smiled on me or when success came my way.

The year I bought the first of my two new cars, I was paying for my first house. I paid in three installments and, by 2012, I was done. It was a two-bedroom detached house at Devtraco Courts in Tema Community 25. I had got to the stage in my life where I felt I had to be on my own. Being on my own and living a life according to my own terms meant that I had to be under my own roof. With that goal in mind, I exerted pressure on myself and worked tirelessly. The movie roles I got from Nigeria paid off and I invested almost all the earnings in that house.

The excitement of owning my own house clouded out sound judgment in the selection of a location for the house. Tema Community 25 is far removed from the centre of the city, but in my desperation to leave Dansoman, I didn't consider this. If I had concerns, those concerns were overwritten by the encouragement from my elder brother, who was also acquiring a property there. I later learnt that he was dating a lady in Tema, so moving there was in line with his plans. The irrational choice of location for my house dawned on me when I moved into the house. Whenever I finished shooting and it was too late in the night, going back was a problem. It was not secure to use the motorway at very odd hours and make the solitary journey off the motorway to my new and secluded neighbourhood. That extended residential area of the industrial city of Tema was not as developed as it is today. I sometimes went back to Dansoman to sleep and continue work the following day. At other times, I spent the nights at a friend's place in East Legon. I soon realised that the problem I intended to solve was still there. After two years, I started to look for a place closer to the centre of Accra, where I plied my trade.

I saved and acquired a three-bedroom house at Redrow Estates at East Legon Hills. This house had a bigger hall and was more secure than my previous place. I was the second to move into this gated estate when it was completed. The first was a French couple. I was so desperate to move that I didn't wait to furnish it before moving in. The surrounding was still a mess, and when it rained, I walked in mud to my house the first few months I moved in. For the sake of convenience, however, I couldn't wait to move in. The estate developer completed my part when I was shooting a movie, so I didn't have the time to pack or transfer the furniture from Tema Community 25. In the beginning, I didn't even have curtains. All I had was a mattress on the floor, and that was good enough for me to move in.

One day, one of the contractors at Devtraco hinted me of a piece of land that was up for sale at East Legon Hills. It took me a year to decide the suitability of the land for the house I intended to build for myself. The indecisiveness also bought me enough time until the Nigerian telecom giant, Glo, signed me as a brand ambassador. I acquired the land and started to build at my own pace and specification to suit my taste. In 2018, it was habitable enough to move in. That is where I have lived up to date.

CHAPTER TEN

Iyanya and My Love Life

My first encounter with love was in the second year of junior secondary school. I fell for Aziz, a boy who joined St. Martin de Porres School from Achimota Basic School. Academically, Aziz was the unserious type. I later gathered that he had been sacked from Achimota Basic School for poor academic performance. That information didn't dent my love for him. What he lacked in books was made up for in entertainment. He was a member of the Fugees and we mounted the stage to perform together.

Aziz was that student who was often punished for the wrong reasons. I was in his circles and it was common to see us punished together for eating in class without cleaning or getting whipped at the assembly for one misbehaviour or the other. He was eventually sacked from St. Martin de Porres School for poor performance. I wept when I got home and the reality dawned on me that I wasn't going to see Aziz again. When asked, I couldn't say the real reason I cried.

Aziz's disregard for books rubbed off on me a great deal, but I managed to pull through with weak grades that were strong enough to grant me admission to Aggrey Memorial, where I met Fianko Bossman, my high school lover. As fate would have it, Fianko was transferred from Aggrey Memorial, but that didn't end our relationship. We continued our teenage love briefly after secondary school and became very good friends afterward. He has been one of the most helpful people I have met in life. In fact, I think everybody needs a Fianko Bossman in their lives. He has such a good heart.

The type of men I have fallen for tells a lot about me. I tend to gravitate towards people's needs, talents, intelligence and realness. Looks or six packs are secondary in my choice of men. I have a strong aversion for older men, what they call sugar daddies. I always feel these are people who have almost finished having fun as far as relationships are concerned and want you as a plaything.

My most significant experiment with love happened with the Nigerian Afropop singer, Iyanya Onoyom Mbuk. It was not strange that from my near-death experience after a brief spell with a musician, I fell in love with another musician. I have already professed my love for music and how gravitating towards musicians came to me as second nature. Part of my acting career was in Nigeria, so it was also natural that our paths crossed.

We had a decent relationship—breakfast in bed and all the niceties of a dream relationship one could think of. I had the assurance that he was someone I could be with forever. He tattooed my initials, YN, on his wrist, and I thought that was a big deal. If he wasn't serious about me, he wouldn't do that. In his hit song, "Ur Waist", he mentioned how he lusted over me. One can therefore imagine my shock when I returned to Ghana after one of my visits to Nigeria and someone called me from his house.

The caller said anytime I left Iyanya's place, another actress came over to him and sometimes slept over. The person felt strongly that there was something going on between them and thought I should know. That actress turned out to be Tonto Dikeh of Nigeria, one of the female celebrities Iyanya named in his "Ur Waist" song. When I was convinced about the authenticity of the information I received, I was heartbroken. I took to Twitter to rant and vent. Tonto Dikeh responded on Twitter, saying people changed and so did feelings, so I should move on.

I later heard more stories about what Iyanya did with some of his female crew members. It convinced me that what happened between him and Tonto Dikeh wasn't an isolated incident. It was a pattern, his way of life. I knew I eventually would have left even if Tonto Dikeh hadn't come into the picture. I did not see the need to keep fighting her for a man I had lost, especially when I knew her fate was not going to be different from mine.

However, it is one thing knowing that there is a good reason to leave and it is another world of hell to accept the decision psychologically and emotionally. It is often easy to convince the mind, but the heart lacks understanding. The heart would often want to be left alone to do things its own way. That was my ordeal during the break up with Iyanya. For two months, I cried inconsolably. A friend of mine got irritated at a point. She didn't understand why a "whole" me would brood so long over a man who had betrayed my love.

My efforts to forget about the issue were undermined by the insane interest the media in Nigeria and Ghana developed in our break-up. They dragged it from our perspective and their own perspective. Those with advanced degrees in relationship management offered their unsolicited opinions, while those who were clothed with the power to administer the morality code of the universe had their say. The storm raged on for a long time and, from time to time, some media outlets still looked back to regurgitate the headlines and find a way of linking the past with unrelated present events.

When I eventually moved on, my next biggest test of love came from another continent. Ghana had not worked. And Nigeria had failed me painfully. I was certain the United Kingdom would work out because everything about Jamie Roberts had the markings of a perfect partner and doting father.

Jamie and I began casually online. He had known me through his Nigerian wife. The woman was not only my fan. People said we looked alike. She was tall, like a model, so I guess she may have started following me because she was told about her striking resemblance with a Ghanaian actress. That's how her husband also got to know me. He reached out through social media and introduced himself as a British photographer whose wife was my fan. After the casual chat, we went silent for a long time.

About a year later, when we got in touch and I asked about his wife, he said things hadn't gone as expected. Their marriage had hit a destructive iceberg and gone cold in broken pieces. He opened up to me and told me a lot about the woman. From how he went on and on about his ex-wife anytime we spoke, I got the impression he hadn't got over her. Months passed and we spoke casually. We got closer as friends, regularly messaging and calling each other.

I told him I would visit anytime I was in London, but he made it easier by proposing to travel to Ghana to see me. He came over. I realised he was very nice. He quickly settled into the Ghanaian environment as if he had lived here all his life. He ate waakye as if he had transitioned from his mother's breast milk with it and had eaten it ever since.

Jamie is a black man in a white man's body. He loves African food, music and, of course, its women. He likes them black and tall. His first wife, with whom he had two children before marrying the Nigerian, was a black South African. I would have been his third African wife had things not ended so quickly and painfully.

Love is difficult to withhold even in the exercise of utmost caution. In other words, if you have suffered a painful heartbreak and you make a mental note never to love with all your heart, that promise only holds until you find someone you truly love. What I had gone through in the past did not dim what I had for Jamie. I gave that relationship my all and he in turn made me feel I was worth the whole world. We got into a serious relationship, and he would turn out to be the father of my daughter, Ryn.

Ryn was supposed to cement our relationship and make things complete. We were supposed to naturally transition from what we had built to a more formal and binding one. He was a man in whom I saw a husband. Having monitored how he related with and treated his two older children, I considered him the ideal father for my kids. But while we planned, his ex-wife had a more elaborate plan. It was her plan that worked to perfection, not ours.

One day, I received an explosive email from Jamie's Nigerian ex-wife. I knew her intention was to destroy him to me, to keep us apart. The email was written in a way that left very little or no room for failure on her part. She knew the effect she wanted to achieve with the email and she got just that.

The email was detailed and explosively explicit. She took her time to reveal all the dirt about her ex-husband, details that would shake any woman no matter how deep her love for a man is. My love for Jamie was deep. It was the reason the email tore us apart. It may sound ironic, but if I hadn't loved him so deeply, our relationship would have continued even after the email. When you love someone with all your heart, they're able to hurt you deeply. And to say I was hurt after reading the email is an understatement. I was broken.

After the email, there were always doubts. There were always questions. The trust was completely gone. I made a decision to opt out of the relationship despite being pregnant for him. It was tough for both of us.

Jamie is still very much present in the life of our daughter. He is one of the most caring fathers I know. Having lived without a father, the last thing I would do is prevent my daughter from enjoying fatherly love. When Jamie visits to see Ryn, I give him the guest room. Sometimes, after a week, he would tell me he is going back.

After Jamie, I lost the essence of falling in love and believing in a man. My worldview about marriage also changed afterwards, and I prefer a partnership to marriage. I believe in partnership, having someone you want and not having to sign a contract. As a woman, I'm trying to work hard and be independent. If marriage is to solve the insecurity of what happens when a man leaves, that doesn't really apply to me now. If you're in love with someone, why do you sign a contract? Signing that contract is like an acknowledgment that it won't work and the marital contract cannot save it. You can sign a contract to be responsible for the kids and for other commitments, but you cannot sign a contract to love someone.

Considering what has become the norm with many marriages, it doesn't make sense to sign a contract. It does not change anything.

CHAPTER ELEVEN

#DumsorMustStop, Akufo-Addo's Call & the Offer to Contest on NPP Ticket

In 2015, a message I considered to be a usual rant on Twitter turned out to be the rallying point for one of the biggest non-partisan protests ever held in Ghana. It was one of the proudest moments of my life, a moment that made my voice heard on the mismanagement of my country and the messy state of affairs in which an otherwise rich nation had found itself. The frustration had been building up in me for many years. When the time was due, it came out naturally and created the needed effect and impact.

My dissatisfaction with my society, country and the black race as a whole started in my childhood. Long before America's culture and lifestyle conscripted me through entertainment, I had begun to compare and question the things that were made in Ghana and those made in Europe, America or Asia. If I bought a pencil here in Ghana and saw another pencil from a classmate whose parent or other relative had returned from the United States or Europe with it as a gift, I compared mine with theirs. Most of the time, the difference was clear. There was always something about the foreign-made product that made the local ones look inferior. There are some who argue that such difference is rooted in the inferiority mindset of the black, but that is not true. The finishing or packaging of the foreign ones stood out. The crude and haphazardly assembled products made here appeared as though the manufacturers here did not care about competition or aesthetics.

As I grew older, I began to see beyond the look and feel of foreign-made products. It began to dawn on me that Ghana, Africa and the black race in general, were helpless and had to look outside for solutions to the most basic problems plaguing them. Attempts to instill empty words and vague slogans of patriotism in the youth did not help change this mentality in me because the reality on the ground was in stark contrast to what my teachers and books said about being black and proud of one's heritage. That reality drowned the hopes of the founding fathers and what, in their days, were considered inspirational rallying calls for the advancement of Africa and the black race.

No child in my days went through basic school without learning about the story of Ghana's independence. And no textbook told that story without the role of Dr. Kwame Nkrumah, the man who led Ghana to independence. Nkrumah is remembered for the profundity of his proclamations, the strength of his convictions and his faith in the black race. I'm unsure whether he carried this optimism to the grave or whether the circumstances surrounding his overthrow and exile taught him that he trusted too much in a people who had no trust in themselves. Known as one of the greatest pan-Africanists to ever live, Nkrumah was fiercely optimistic about Africa's ability to take charge of its destiny and prove a point to the rest of the world.

On the eve of Ghana's independence, he declared that "the independence of Ghana is meaningless unless it is linked up with total liberation of the African continent." His quest for a united Africa, which took a life of its own in the Nkrumah era, was personified in these words.

For his faith in the black race, Dr. Nkrumah declared on that night: "But also, as I pointed out, that also entails hard work. That new Africa is ready to fight her own battles and show that, after all, the black man is capable of managing his own affairs."

As a child growing up and learning these words, I soon came to the realisation that they were empty slogans, especially because the first part that talked about hard work is often left out in both Nkrumah's quote and the endeavours of the black continent. I was born two decades after Nkrumah left the political scene in Ghana. However, I have learned a few of the things he did to practicalise the words he so eloquently declared on the night the Union Jack was lowered. In its place, the Red, Yellow, and Green with the Black Star was hoisted proudly and it fluttered audaciously with the promise of a new nation.

After Nkrumah and his generation, however, there has not been much evidence to prove that the black man—whether in Africa or the diaspora— is capable of managing his own affairs. Sometimes, I genuinely hope that I am wrong. I hope that I am too pessimistic. The reality, however, often defeats any attempt I make at optimism.

For instance, Ghana is among the world's leading producers of cocoa and gold and is home to a host of other natural minerals and fertile soil. However, we have no say in the value chain of the raw materials we produce. We still export raw cocoa beans and get next to nothing from the multi-billion-dollar chocolate industry. Our gold is mostly mined by foreign companies and refined abroad. When we struck oil in commercial quantities, we lacked the economic and technical capacities to exploit it, so we looked up to the West, and, as usual, our percentage in it is negligible when compared to the countries whose companies are mining the oil. When politicians talk about adding value to our farm produce and moving beyond an agrarian economy to an industrial one, they are almost always in opposition. In government, they are too occupied with amassing wealth for themselves and their descendants to think about the lofty ideas they espoused when they were hungry for power.

Dictated by their insatiable greed and consumed by their selfish interests, our leaders sign some of the worst contracts when they have the opportunity to negotiate on our behalf. The little revenue we derive from our resources are often misused, leaving too little with which to provide critical social needs and infrastructure.

In an era when our Asian counterparts who were like us at independence are miles ahead of us, we do not seem to have any concrete plans to make us competitive on the global stage. We have no sense of urgency. Our education is still a relic of our colonial past. Our lawyers and judges still wear *white* wigs and are compelled to be fully robed in the blistering heat when very few of the courtrooms outside the national capital have air-conditioners or proper ventilation.

Despite our enormous human resources, we seem to contribute nothing to the world of science and invention. The black men and women who have stood out have done so on the fertile grounds of innovation created for them in America or Europe. Back home, we tend to hold fast to cultural practices that add nothing to our humanity and progress. I have always expressed these frustrations to friends and we would rant and conclude that the solution is not rocket science.

The greed that made us willingly sell our own race to others in the Trans-Atlantic Slave Trade is still the creed in most African countries. It is in our DNA. So, I sometimes ask myself: if I were that *white man*, what would I make of blacks and their nations that are beggars? What respect would I have for a continent that is endowed with resources, but is so hopelessly helpless that when disaster strikes, its default position is to look to others for salvation? If we flipped the coin, would we genuinely think that we deserve the same amount of respect that should be accorded people of other races and continents, those who continue to make advances while we kill one another in greed-induced civil wars?

Most of the time, the voices that speak up against our failure and bad governance are those of academics, political activists and civil society groups. The discourse in Ghana, however, got into unconventional circles and the frustration got to every lip between 2013 and 2015, when erratic power supply disrupted every sphere of life and threatened to further undermine the little progress we had made. A nation of nearly 30 million people was still relying mainly on the hydropower systems constructed by the Kwame Nkrumah administration when the population of the nation was less than 8 million. When the power crises persisted, the pinch became so severe that even the most passive observers became active participants in our discourse.

The politics of "dumsor" dominated media discussions. The name of the recurring phenomenon of unstable power supply, dumsor, is derived from two Twi words—"dum," meaning "switch off", and "sɔ", meaning "switch on". Dumsor wasn't new, but the one recorded in that period is the worst in living memory.

I am not an expert on energy, governance or economics, so my frustration with the power crises was mostly with friends and people in my circles. But one night, I was compelled to take my ranting to Twitter when I was tired of buying diesel to power my generator set. Besides the heat I had to endure in the absence of electricity, my health was also at risk.

I use Xalacom eyedrop, which needs refrigeration. I have a family history of glaucoma, and that medication, according to information available online, is meant to reduce "intraocular pressure (IOP) in patients with open-angle glaucoma and ocular hypertension". I had to refrigerate the medication and since the national grid was almost always off, I had to keep the generator on. The cost of fuel was draining me financially. My most pressing need for an uninterrupted supply of power was to store medication. There were others whose very livelihoods depended on electricity.

It was for this reason that when I tweeted my frustration and ended with #DumsorMustStop, I woke up the following morning to find that the hashtag had caught fire on Twitter and was trending for days on end.

In the midst of the trend, the Citizen Ghana Movement pressure group reached out to me. They wanted to discuss how we could capitalise on the mood generated by my hashtag to pile greater pressure on the government to fix the problem. I met with leaders of the pressure group, lawyers Kofi Bentil and Nana Kwasi Awuah. The two had broken away from the OccupyGhana pressure group, which was the outcome of a non-partisan protest in 2014. I bought into their idea and they set to work on the legal requirements ahead of what became the #DumsorMustStop protest.

On my part, I reached out to all the celebrities I knew and sold the idea of the protest to them. It was an opportunity for those of us in the arts and entertainment industry to make our voices count, but not many of them responded. I was, however, happy that the few who came on board did so wholeheartedly. They included Efya Nocturnal, Van Vicker, D-Black, Prince David Osei, DKB, Kweku Elliot and Sarkodie. Sarkodie could not make it to the protest, but he recorded a hit song about the power crises.

It was normal that a problem of that magnitude would give a political advantage to the opposition political parties, so while the government did not take kindly to our protest, the opposition parties were solidly behind us even though we had made it clear that our agenda was non-partisan. In the days leading up to the protest, I received a call from someone who said I should hold on for the presidential candidate of the opposition New Patriotic Party (NPP), Nana Addo Dankwa Akufo-Addo. In that brief call, he expressed his support for my cause and encouraged me. He said I was a true daughter of the land and that what I was doing was a good thing. He said I should push on and not be discouraged, for the whole of Ghana was behind me.

I also received calls from the office of President John Dramani Mahama. The callers said the president wanted to meet me, but I told them I would only meet with the president on condition that my fellow organisers of the protest would be part of that meeting. The officials at the presidency insisted that the president wanted to meet me alone. I stood my ground, stating that if the president was not prepared to meet me with my colleagues, then the meeting was not going to happen.

And it did not happen.

A few days before the protest, there was pressure from my family members, who tried to talk me out of it. I remember my father, Mr. Nelson, called me one morning and, without even greeting me, asked me to drop the protest. He said the Nelson name had become embroiled in a national controversy because of my intended action.

"Yvonne, the name. The name! The name!" he said and went ahead to tell me how his friends were calling him to talk to me.

It was interesting that the man who didn't make me feel part of him suddenly became so concerned about me when I was embarking on a national cause. I still wonder how the people who were influential enough to want to stop the protest were able to link me to Mr. Nelson and put him under such intense pressure that he called me. Our relationship as father and daughter was not out there in the public. I had thought it was as anonymous as how we related with each other until Mr. Nelson called. I declined to recline and watch the nation suffer when I had the unique opportunity to make my voice heard.

That evening, my mother also called with the same plea. It was either Mr. Nelson had told her to add her voice to dissuade me from leading the protest or she was genuinely concerned for my security and the implications of leading a crowd in the politically charged environment. Whatever her motivation was, I politely told her that it was too late to reconsider my decision to lead the protest.

The week leading to the protest was my busiest. While putting finishing touches to the arrangement and fending off attempts to stop it, I was also engaged in countless media interviews. I remember brushing my teeth in the car one morning while on my way to an early in-studio radio interview at Peace FM. It was as if I was running a political campaign.

May 16, 2015, finally arrived as a very tense day. My team and I had done a lot of preparation, but we could not be sure that Ghanaians would turn out in their numbers to make the protest a success. The government and the governing party were doing everything possible to undermine the protest. It was supposed to be a vigil, and participants were asked to bring their lanterns and candles to march from the University of Ghana to the Tetteh Quarshie Interchange. The Minister of Power, Dr. Kwabena Donkor, later told me that his outfit fixed the dysfunctional streetlights on that stretch just to douse the effect we wanted to create with the thousands of lanterns and other lights we used for the protest. Keyboard gangs of the governing party were also ready to undertake their coordinated trolling should the numbers fall short of their expectation. The stakes were high. They knew it. And we knew it.

When the moment came, I was overwhelmed and moved by the numbers that turned out. Tens of thousands of protestors from different walks of life turned out. Some people travelled in buses from Kumasi to Accra to take part in the protest. The Ghanaian media gave it live coverage, while the international media featured it prominently in their news. Social media was awash with our messages and pictures and live streams of the event. We made a strong statement. It became the most significant and defining moment for the fight to end the power crises in Ghana.

As with all actions against the government, the protest came at a cost to my comfort and security. I received anonymous death threats from people who felt I was making the government unpopular. Two weeks after the protest, I didn't sleep in my house. While away, a neighbour once called me and said some Toyota SUVs had parked outside my home and their occupants were peering into my compound. But for the high wall, I guess they might have entered. The gated residential community where I lived at the time came under intense scrutiny. The estate developer was accused of not having electricity metres in some of the apartments and was arrested and detained. I had a metre so no matter how hard they looked, they couldn't find anything to implicate or incriminate me. After some time, they left me alone, and I returned home.

A year later, the opposition NPP and its candidate won the 2016 election. The power crisis and its effects were a major sin of the incumbent National Democratic Congress (NDC). Dumsor had resulted in job losses and dealt a deadly blow to the small-scale enterprises that depended on electricity but could not afford alternative sources of power. Even though the NDC administration resolved the crises at a huge cost and through shady procurement deals, the victims of dumsor, corruption and mismanagement could not forgive the party at the presidential and parliamentary polls. The NPP, led by Nana Addo Dankwa Akufo-Addo, won massively in both the presidential and parliamentary elections.

Some friends and I went to congratulate the president-elect, Nana Akufo-Addo, with whom we took a photograph. It is a photograph I regret taking. Akufo-Addo came to the presidency with enormous goodwill. He had been projected as a no-nonsense disciplinarian who would not hesitate to crack the whip on errant appointees. He was said to be incorruptible, and Ghanaians thought he was going to be the antidote to mass stealing at the highest level, which is euphemised as corruption. Unfortunately for Ghana and those who trusted in him, he has turned out to be a monumental disappointment whose government's unbridled borrowing, corruption and reckless spending plunged the nation into an economic dumsor.

By the end of the first term of Akufo-Addo's presidency, many Ghanaians had begun to lose hope, not only in him but also in the country and its politics. It was not strange that his party nearly lost the parliamentary majority it commanded in the first term. There was a tie in the parliamentary polls. The NPP only got the majority when its member who had been expelled from the party from contesting the election as an independent candidate, won his seat and joined the NPP side in parliament. Even with that, the governing party lost the election of the Speaker of Parliament for the first time in Ghana's Fourth Republic. I certainly do not wish to associate with a politician who is projected as one thing but becomes the polar opposite of that

121

when elected into office. Strangely, however, some close associates of the president thought I was a candidate to be drafted into their party and pushed to contest a parliamentary seat with their tacit endorsement and support.

Prior to the 2020 polls, an influential man in the Akufo-Addo circles came to see me and proposed to sponsor me to contest the Ayawaso West Wuogon parliamentary seat on the ticket of the NPP. The NPP had lost its MP for the area and one of the "wives" of the late MP won the byelection in 2019. The byelection was characterised by violence and resulted in the formation of a commission of enquiry to investigate it. She was lacing her boots to contest the seat in 2020. When I drew the attention of the emissary to the fact that the party already had a candidate, he said the fact that he was contacting me meant that they had concluded their plans and would do everything within their power to pave the way for me to contest if only I was interested.

I asked him to give me a couple of days to think about it, but I had made up my mind the moment he broached the subject. I was not interested in the offer. Even if I was interested in going to parliament, who told him I wanted to do that on the ticket of the NPP? What if I wanted to go as an independent candidate? And was I going to allow myself to be someone's political puppet? Once you accept to be sponsored by them, you lose your independence and they expect unalloyed loyalty from you. This was something I wouldn't do even if I was interested. This person was the president's family member. And from the modus operandi of the Akufo-Addo "family and friends" government, I wasn't going to be their conduit, even if I was interested in going to parliament.

Apart from the fact that they probably saw a formidable political personality in me as a result of the #DumsorMustStop protest, the other reason the NPP's gods wanted me to contest was not difficult to discern. My colleague actor and friend, John Dumelo, was contesting that constituency on the ticket of the opposition NDC and they feared he could unseat the NPP candidate with his celebrity status. Already, John Dumelo's political affiliation had strained our friendship. We had had open exchanges on Twitter in the past and I wasn't going to make things worse by openly contesting him. I wouldn't betray our friendship to satisfy some people's political calculations. If I accepted the offer, I was going to do that because of the convenience of political power.

That constituency is a stronghold of the NPP, the main reason John Dumelo lost despite his popularity and stardom. If I had contested, my chances of winning would have been high, but I do not regret rejecting the offer. Had I accepted that offer, I wouldn't be different from the politicians and their politics of convenience, which I so much detested.

Miss Ghana 2005:
I step out in style
in my swimwear

*Receiving the best talent award
from Prince Kofi Amoabeng*

*During one of the speech
segments at Miss Ghana*

*The contestants meet President J.A. Kufuor at the Osu Castle,
the then seat of government. I am third from the left*

The perfect five from which the final three winners were selected

126

On the set of Play Boy, from left to right: Jackie Appiah, Ingrid Alabi, Henry, myself and Beverly Afaglo

On the set of Fantasia with Rita Dominic, Director Anuka, I and Van Vicker

Emeka Ike and I [seated] on a set in Lagos

I, Asantewaa [in the middle] and Jackie Appiah at an event in Accra

Majid, Frank Raja [middle] and I on set

In Lagos filming with Eucharia Anunobi

With Genevieve Nnaji on set in Lagos

"I attracted more movie roles from other producers and I started starring in movies that had me as the main character or the only big-name character driving the movie. The movies I featured in after Princess Tyra are Passion and Soul..."

In this photo , I was on set filming Passion and Soul

"*Of hostilities on set, I must say I also felt very comfortable whenever I was on set with Majid Michel...*"

With Enebeli Elebuwa on the set of Fantasia, a Ghanaian movie.

In Lagos filming Chidi Mokeme

Kofi Adjorlolo walked out of the set of Princess Tyra as a protest against what he termed as my terrible acting. We later became friends and I even cast him in a movie I produced.

With Majid

With Desmond Elliot in Ghana

"The release of Princess Tyra changed everything. My status at home changed. My brother and sister now saw me as a celebrity sister. The posters of celebrities that littered the walls of my room were still there, but the disdain that had accompanied them vanished overnight."

With Viva Bianca, an American actress in Santa Barbara in Los Angeles in the filming of Road to Redemption

With Akon

My third time as a movie director

With John Dumelo on the set of Jungle Justice

*I found directing so
interesting that I wish
I had started earlier*

*Shooting a commercial
for Brussels Airlines in
2022*

With lawyers Nana Kwasi Awuah (left) and Kofi Bentil after we got clearance from the police to proceed with the protest.

The #DumsorMustStop protest was a huge success. It shook the government to the core.

This was one of the interviews in which I said Mr. Nelson was not in my life

CHAPTER TWELVE

A Man's World

In 2009, when I was on set shooting *The Prince's Bride*, I received a visitor. He was not my visitor, for he had come there to see someone else. By the end of his visit, however, I turned out to matter more to him than the person he had come to see. This august visitor, if I should call him so because of the retinue of security guards he moved with, derived his influence from the surname he carried. His name is Joel Duncan-Williams, the son of the founder and leader of the Action Faith Chapel International, Archbishop Nicholas Duncan-Williams. Until that day, I hadn't known or heard about him, but I could not fail to notice his imposing presence when he showed up.

Before he left where we were shooting the movie, he said he had fallen in love with me. The days and weeks that followed proved he was not joking. He would buy me lunch and visit me on set. I was amused by his security and the mini-convoy that followed him. I began to wonder what threats he encountered that warranted the kind of escort he moved with. While I was still unsure of what to tell him, his plans were far advanced for marriage. But something ended our friendship abruptly before it had the slimmest probability of developing beyond that.

He paid me a visit one evening with the usual princely entourage that I had only seen in movies of non-state officials. When the howling of his motorcade's siren had adequately announced to the neighbourhood that my household had received an important somebody, he came in and announced his plans. He said, before the marriage would proceed, I had to go to his father to be prayed for. The purpose of that prayer was to ensure that whatever demons or evil spirits were present in me or my family line would be cast out. In my head, I asked whether he didn't think my mother also needed to pray to cast out any potential bad spirits in him. Being the son of Archbishop Duncan-Williams didn't necessarily mean he was inhabited by the Holy Spirit and guarded by angels. And who told him that being an actress meant that I was a harbinger of malevolent spirits?

At least, those who lived in our area would testify that the Manovia household used to be one of the most religious households around. My mother's sense of spirituality heightened after a motor accident she was involved in, and it was rare to miss morning devotion in our house. Those were the times, in my teen years, I used to interrupt prayer sessions with revelations from God. When I started my acting career,

I made it a point to always pray before I started any movie role I was given. I am not one of those who wear their religion on their sleeves, but I believe in God and believe in prayers. I have seen the hand of God in my affairs many times and I have no doubt He comes through for me when I call on Him. I don't believe in just big pastors or men of God, some of whom are nothing short of entrepreneurs. I, therefore, found it funny that someone who was interested in marrying me and hadn't secured my consent thought I needed to be spiritually cleansed even before he proceeded. He didn't see the need for that cleansing to be mutual.

Outside the realm of spirituality, that thinking betrays a certain mindset that I have come to see in a lot of men, especially in Ghana and Nigeria—terrains I'm familiar with. It is a mindset that reinforces the unfortunate reality that this is a man's world. It is an entitlement mindset that a woman must be subservient to a man and be subject to his wishes and dictates. It is an unwritten rule that expects a woman to be complementary to a man and that her own priorities and feelings must be subsumed by the overriding ambitions of the man. In the case of Joel Duncan-Williams, it was evident that he was thinking about one side, his side and his interests. Others have a cruder way of manifesting this mindset. It is the forceful entitlement to women's bodies. I knew it existed, but the movie industry opened my eyes to its pervasiveness and seriousness

When a popular movie director in Ghana threatened not to cast me in a movie again unless I gave in to his sexual demands, I initially didn't take it seriously. I thought it was just an empty threat that was meant to put pressure on a fame-hungry young woman. But he meant it, and, for a year, he did not look my way in the movies that came from his stable. He had made the advances for a long time, and when it became clear to him that I would not yield, he wielded the ultimate trump card. He tossed a sack of juicy hay in front of a young woman foraging for the foliage of success and fame and all the trappings that came with it. I didn't accept the poisonous bait, so he carried out his threat. After a year, he was convinced that he had failed and because he needed my service, he came back to make peace with me. But I had to give something else to placate him. I ended up acting in a number of movies for him for free. In all, I have done about fifteen movies without charging a fee. I needed to stay visible, relevant and be in the trends. The more movies one shot, the more one stayed in the minds of people and had the potential of landing juicier offers. Producers know this, and women who are now looking for the opportunity to enter the industry are often required to exchange sex for roles.

Was I shocked that this director went this far to punish me for something I had the right to refuse anyone I had no feelings for?

Not at all.

If what he did had any effect on me, it only confirmed that I was born into a man's world. I had to live with it and endure the consequences if I could not change it. That world influenced me a great deal even before I became conscious of it. As I've already stated elsewhere in this book, the male-dominated hip-hop culture shaped my early life. It's the reason I grew up as a tomboy. I loved it. I also grew up naturally drifting more towards men than women. I felt more comfortable around men than women and that meant I learnt the ways of men very early in life. The more I knew, the more hopeless I became of the reality of women in a world they dominate only in numbers. I have always been around men, but I couldn't think like men or behave like them. I am a woman. And they are men. I feel if we got into the same trouble, society would judge them more leniently than me.

Men get away with a lot of things, or so I think. They control a lot of things in the world and dictate the pace and sometimes the phases of women's lives. They vastly outnumber their female counterparts in every industry. In entertainment, a woman needs more than just talent to succeed. A woman needs to be mentally tough, principled and ever ready to suffer for not yielding to the demands of every Tom, *Dick* and Harry.

Nature itself has placed uncomfortable and—sometimes disconcerting—restrictions on women. Think about menstruation. Think about menopause. (As if to remind us about men's dominance, those words begin with men.) Some women's periods are so painful that it is a dreaded monthly burden. At 60, a man can still have children. After 30, a woman who wants to have children begins to be restless and pressured because as she inches towards 50, her chances of conceiving begin to dim. Pregnancy comes with its complications. Sometimes, it

142

is a life-or-death affair, which is borne by the woman. Nature's burden weighs disproportionately against women.

Aside from the minority that are able to hire paid house helps and an even slimmer minority whose men help them at home, household chores still remain the burden of women. A man can go to work a day after the birth of his child, but a woman must first heal. She must breastfeed and act as the primary caretaker of the baby. In some instances, as in my case, the career of the woman must be put on hold when she's pregnant. She must watch helplessly and painfully as opportunities slip by or are taken away from her.

This dominance finds a disturbing expression in marriage as well. A woman is often in the shadows of a man. It is becoming normal for men to cheat, but sacrilegious for women to do so, and I wonder the essence of marriage when the two parties are not held to the same standards of the so-called hallowed institution of God. Sometimes, I'm tempted to think men are wired differently. Being around men, I have realised that a man can be with 20 women in a given year, and that's absolutely fine with him. Many women who enter into relationships or marriages with their hearts often end up disappointed; and when they have to leave, a majority of them do not get a share of the property that is proportionate to their sweat.

In all of this, my main frustration has been the sense of entitlement some men wield over women who are neither their children nor wives. As I grew in the industry, I discovered that despite the talent of a woman, the average producer or movie director would want to take advantage of her sexually before she is allowed to flourish. That is a disturbing reality, and not many women are able to turn their backs on the offers. I was fortunate that I entered the movie industry after the Miss Ghana contest, which had given me some clout before I starred in my first movie.

I know, as women, we have our own issues, but if we had women in the majority as producers and directors, I don't think they would be making these demands of men. I can't imagine refusing to cast a talented actor because he will not sleep with me. Sadly, women who yield to the demands of their producers are not spared harassment by the entertainment media. When they appear for interviews, they are asked about it. Even their normal relationships are scrutinised and made to take the centre stage in discussions when they appear on media platforms for interviews to promote their work.

In my case, I had been featured in a number of good movies and I was sought after. Besides my stubborn-spirited opposition to bullies, I had options so I didn't struggle to fend off the *no-sex, no-role* rule in the industry. As I grew in the industry and basked in stardom, I learnt that the sense of entitlement was not limited to men who employed women. There were men who think by virtue of their position, wealth or influence, you should be at their beck and call. Some of them are men for whom society has the highest respect, men who are regarded as paragons of righteousness.

144

There is a renowned pastor in Ghana who has made conquering me part of his mission. He is not out to conquer me for the Lord, but for himself. He is married. He has the influence and the money. And his main catchline has been that I should name whatever I wanted. He talks as if I cannot work for my own money. These experiences are not unique to me. They are routine in the industry. Female celebrities are suffering. If you do not yield, you will suffer. If you yield, you suffer all the same.

Sometimes, the pressure and punishment, as in the case of the director who refused me roles because I declined sex, are designed to put fear in young women. But if I were in any position to advise young entrants to the movie or showbiz industry in general, I would say it pays to stand your ground. It pays to work hard and hone your craft and let it speak for you. If you like any man in the industry and you want to date or sleep with him, fair game. That man can even be your producer. You should have a say in whom you decide to get intimate with. It should be your decision. You must, however, learn to say "no" to demeaning demands. Giving yourself out cheaply for a role will eventually hurt you. The industry would soon know that you're malleable to the ravenous and insatiable vultures in there. And by the time they're done with you, you might not even recognise yourself.

My experience with men hasn't been all negative. There are men who have influenced me positively and supported me without demanding sex in return. It isn't always about money or material support. There are people who add value to your life, through the richness of the

145

conversation they share with you. They shape your thinking and challenge you to reach heights you thought were impossible.

I met a man called Samuel Afari Dartey after Miss Ghana. It has been close to two decades and we're still friends. He has influenced my life immensely. Hanging out and talking to him is as if you're attending a career or life-coaching seminar. He has taught me to be focused, endure pain, and think differently. He doesn't understand why a man or woman should change and think the same way as their partners. To him, they are different individuals with different backgrounds. He opened my mind to different things. He is a male friend who did not come in to take advantage of me but has touched my life more than any educational institution has. I cherish and hold such men dear. Of course, he can be brutal. He holds certain weird perspectives that I find over the top, but his experiences and knowledge have shaped me a great deal.

Men like Samuel Afari Dartey are in the minority. Whatever the case, a woman should not give up fighting and creating opportunities that would save other women from falling prey to debauched men who must have their way because they decide who gets featured in a movie or produced on a record label. Starting my own production company may not have crossed my mind had I not faced these challenges very early in my career. It's tough, but we have to fight on.

146

CHAPTER THIRTEEN

Nigeria and Its Powerful Men

Nigeria means many things to many people. To many Ghanaian actors, however, it means a career breakthrough. I am a living testimony of that breakthrough. *Princess Tyra* paved the way for me to enter Nollywood, Nigeria's movie industry. Ghana's Abdul Salam Mumuni and Nigeria's Kingsley Okereke of Divine Touch Productions were friends who sometimes collaborated in their productions. Because *Princess Tyra* was a huge success in Ghana, there was a decision to have a Nigerian version. It was titled *Royalty* and starred Oge Okoye as the lead actor. After that movie, I landed a role in a movie that had Genevieve Nnaji in the cast. It was a dream come true to be cast in the same movie with Genevieve, but I didn't have enough time to revel in that rare glory. A flurry of roles in Nollywood came knocking. At a point, I contemplated putting my education on hold in pursuit of money and fame. It was a thought I dismissed as soon as I formed it, but the fact that it crossed my mind meant the opportunities in Nigeria were extremely tempting.

Beyond the well-paying roles in a much more developed and bigger movie industry, Nigeria presented me with a cultural shock. Ghana and Nigeria aren't supposed to be too different. As the two leading anglophone nations in the West African sub-region, we have a lot in common. We still fight over who prepares the best jollof rice and when our national football teams meet, we treat it like a World Cup final. This rivalry notwithstanding, the entertainment industry has become a melting pot for the two countries. You can hardly attend a party in Ghana without hearing a song by a Nigerian artiste. Ghanaian artists also enjoy considerable acceptance in Nigeria.

On the political front, Ghana and Nigeria haven't been much different. We are dogged by the same issues of bad leadership, corruption and nepotism. Our countries have been hijacked by a few self-seeking and half-baked elites who dominate the political landscape from one election to the other. Corruption is our common denominator, and hopelessness among the vastly youthful populations of our two countries is an ever-growing phenomenon. For these and other reasons, a Ghanaian shouldn't feel too shocked when in Nigeria. But Nigeria shocked me to the core.

In Nigeria, money rules. And everything else must obey without question. If you don't have money, they don't laugh at your jokes. Spray money, and that's when you get attention. Cars and houses define your status. I'm not suggesting that money is bad. And I'm not saying some of these things don't happen in Ghana. But if it is 100 in Ghana and you think you've seen the peak, you are likely to encounter 10, 000 in Nigeria. Nigeria operates on a different level.

When my career took me there, I had to work within it even if I couldn't fit in. Opting out was no option. The movie industry in Nigeria is far bigger than that of Ghana, and no Ghanaian producer ever paid me anything close to what I earned in Nigeria. To keep my job and flow with the industry, I had to learn to appease my audience and hosts without losing myself and my values in the avalanche of demands that teemed my way.

Nigerians understand hyping and would go to all lengths to invest in it. If there's hype around you, they'll come around. Money is the fuel that stokes the hype of people who have nothing much to offer. In such people, the followers do not look at the substance. If you have money but nothing up there, people will still worship you. As an actress in my prime, the quest for brand association made my work in Nigeria extra difficult. A budding actress once took my script and posed with me on set just to post on social media that she was shooting a movie with me, when, in fact, she was nowhere near the cast. I wondered whether her social media followers would not expect to see the movie. But in this make-believe industry, some people would do anything to court fame.

There were people who held parties and were prepared to pay you to attend just to enhance their status or show their class. The array of celebrities that attended someone's party showed who they were. Being present at someone's birthday or some other celebratory event sometimes paid me more than acting in a movie in Ghana.

What made life difficult was the pressure from my circle of friends, some of whom wanted to hang out with me at times I was too tired to party. I often worked deep into the night, and when I was burned out, some friends would want to hang out with me at nightclubs. Some of them would still be sleeping the following morning when I had to wash down and start shooting. I had to strike a difficult balance between my schedule and being able to live in such a way that I wouldn't be seen as snobbish or unsociable. Such tagging came with its own consequences.

Aside from the random friends, especially females who just needed company, my days in Nigeria exposed me to its powerful men in politics, chieftaincy and the church. They were men who thought because of their wealth and influence, they were entitled to you. They mostly used your friends and people in your circles as points of contact. Call such intermediaries pimps and you won't be wrong. I had experienced some of these men in Ghana, but Nigeria is always a notch higher and sometimes scary. I encountered many of these powerful men in my acting days in Nigeria, but a few stood out.

There is a very popular and powerful charismatic preacher in Nigeria who expressed interest in me. I cannot say how he knew I was in Nigeria at that time, but I suppose my actress friend who told me he wanted to meet me was perhaps feeding him with updates about me.

She only said someone wanted to see me and when I went out to see who it was, I was greeted by this popular "man of God". He was calm and everything about him showed that I should have known what he wanted and kotowed to his wishes. I didn't give in. And he wasn't aggressive. After a couple of failed attempts, he gave up and I never heard from him again until I started reading hordes of stories about allegations of sexual assault against him.

Another time, an actress friend told me his uncle wanted to meet me. I told her I had a long day and wouldn't close early, but she had all the patience in the world for me that day. She came and parked her Range Rover and waited until I finished shooting after 11 p.m. Nigeria was scary and driving that late at night was a risk, but she made it sound as though we were going for an important business gig, so I obliged. She picked me up and it was midnight when we got to the Eko Hotel, where the supposed uncle was.

The said uncle of my friend was in the luxurious Signature Suite. She introduced him to me as a popular governor or senator of one of the states in Nigeria. She then went to the lounge of the suite and left me with him in the room. There was no chair in the room, something that seemed deliberate. I sat on the edge of the bed and the most awkward silence I can remember in my life ensued. He, perhaps, had the impression that I knew what to do or say, which I found ridiculous. That wasn't all there was to the drama.

There was a fourth person in the lounge. The politician went to speak briefly to him and came back to tell me the man was his doctor, and that I should give him my blood sample for an HIV test. He said it was just a prick and that everything would be done in a short time. I found it disrespectful and shocking. Even if I wanted to sleep with him, that alone was enough to put any normal woman off. If he was interested in knowing my HIV status, why did he think I would not be interested in his?

I told him that was not the reason I came there and that I wasn't going to do any test. I was calm but firm, though afraid. There were two men and two women in the suite, but the other woman was on the side of the two men, so I was alone. If things got out of hand, I was going to be on my own. I later found out that the man was not her uncle as she had claimed, but she knew why he wanted to see me. When he realised he wasn't going to have his way, he muttered something to my friend to the effect that I was acting weird. Soon, we were on our way out of the hotel. For our "transportation" back home, he gave my friend some dirty Naira notes he had produced from the briefcase that lay on the bed in the room. It was 1 million Naira and my friend gave me half of it. When I later googled his name and saw his photographs and association with a number of female actors and celebrities, I wondered what happened before or after those photographs.

Years later, my curiosity about the politician I had met in the hotel piqued when a Nigerian friend in Ghana told me he had gone to him for a contract but failed to secure it. In the discussion, he revealed that the politician belonged to a cult and had insisted that joining that cult was a prerequisite to doing business with my friend. My friend said he couldn't join, so he cut all ties with him. I have since been thinking about whether the blood sample he wanted to take of me was actually for an HIV test or for something that had to do with his occult business. But that was not going to be my last encounter with powerful men in Nigeria.

The one that turned out to be the scariest of them all was initiated here in Ghana and ended up in the palace of a powerful traditional ruler in Nigeria. I didn't know the traditional ruler who wanted to see me, but the man who told me about him said he knew me and would be instrumental in supporting my Glaucoma Foundation. The foundation was dear to my heart because my grandmother had lost her sight before she passed. I had loved her dearly, and, growing up, I thought she had not been given enough care.

When she had glaucoma and went to the Korle-Bu Teaching Hospital, she didn't get enough education, so she used the eyedrop for a month and stopped. When she was almost losing her sight and went back for a surgery, we later learnt there was gross negligence on the part of those who carried out the operation. Her condition became irreversible. When she passed, I was in senior high school and felt I hadn't reciprocated the love she had shown me. It was one of the saddest days in my life. She was all I had as an extended family member. I felt my mother had not paid much attention to her eyesight.

I AM NOT YVONNE NELSON

Later, my mother had a problem with her eyes and went to the hospital. When the specialists investigated our family history of glaucoma, they realised my mother and I had what they called high pressures in our eyes. Deep in my heart, the foundation was in the memory of the woman I dearly loved and I hoped that through it, many others would have their sights saved. When the man told me how the Nigerian traditional ruler was supportive of charities such as mine, I was happy to meet him and tell him what I wanted to do with the Yvonne Nelson Glaucoma Foundation.

From Accra, we flew to Lagos and boarded another flight to the traditional ruler's home state. The turbulence on that flight is the most violent I have ever experienced. At one point, I thought the worst was about to happen. At that point, I began to regret embarking on the trip. When we survived what appeared to me like a near crash, I hoped something extra-ordinarily useful would come out of that trip to offset the torture I had endured. It steeled me against any possible nonsense before we got to the palace. The palace was a magnificent castle. One had to go through several halls before coming face-to-face with the ruler. Wait here. Come here. Go there. These were the instructions I heard until I met the powerful ruler, who was not so powerful in physique.

He was a frail old man who looked like someone who could not survive another five years. The inner court I was ushered in to meet him had a magnificent royal bed, where he beckoned me to join him. Whatever the intermediary had told me did not happen. The traditional ruler was not interested in my foundation. He was not interested in my career or anything I was doing. He didn't even deem it necessary to strike up a conversation with me. It seemed, like the governor, this old man expected me to know why I was there. He expected me to go ahead and act on cue. I had prepared to resist anything untoward and his attitude fortified my resolve even more. When he asked me to join him on the bed, I wondered what he needed me there for. At his age, what was he up to? I didn't move. And when he realised he had made a wrong choice, he dismissed me.

He gave the man who took me there a wad of dollar notes, who then gave me a share of $5000 as compensation for travelling to see the king. I was so angry with him that we ceased to be friends upon my return from that trip. He organises an awards ceremony that is well-patronised and I wonder whether pimping for powerful men is part of his job. If it is, then in my case, he got the wrong target. I used to respect him because of the kind of people who patronised his programmes. I had known him back in my university days because he was dating my friend.

In the encounters with the powerful Nigerian men, one thing surprised me above all others. The intermediaries did not ever tell me the expectations at the other end. Somehow, they assumed that once a big and powerful man wanted to see you, you were old enough to know what they wanted and should submit to them. It is one of the worst insults to womanhood and one can only imagine the rate of success that keeps them motivated to continue to explore.

CHAPTER FOURTEEN

Genevieve Nnaji and the Rest

There cannot be a movie industry without women. The Ghanaian and Nigerian movie industries have had women of different eras who defined filmmaking in different roles. I have plied my trade in these two countries and I know how instrumental women are to the survival of the movie industry. I also had a brief taste of the movie industry in Cote d'Ivoire. The Ivorian industry was much smaller than those of Ghana and Nigeria, and the language barrier cuts the Francophone movies almost completely from the Anglophone countries in West Africa. In my prime, however, I was privileged to attract interest from film producers in Ghana's western neighbour. In Cote d'Ivoire, it was difficult for me because I do not speak French. When I was cast in French movies, the other characters spoke French while I spoke English. Later, my lines were voiced over so that the entire movie came out in French. That was a short spell, and I don't have as many tales about women in the Ivorian movie industry as I do about Ghana and Nigeria.

The movie industry is full of preys and predators. I have already spoken about how men who wield cash and influence tend to decide who rises to fame and who fails. As I progressed, however, I realised women in the industry were not only vulnerable prey in the hands of perverse men. Some were actually predators who terrorised mostly their fellow women, young women who looked up to them. I saw a bit of that in Ghana, but my worst experience was in Nigeria.

Princess Tyra had opened doors, windows and chimneys for me, and Nigeria came knocking very early in that career. I cannot say enough how Nigeria's Nollywood was the mainstay of many actors from Ghana. It came with fame and exposure to a much bigger audience than Ghana, but the money was the real deal. I remember at a point, some Ghanaian actors moved to settle in Nigeria as roles upon roles beckoned them. The cash trapped them.

I didn't want to be in their faces 24/7, so I made it a point never to relocate to Nigeria. I would go and work there and return. My decision was partly because I found Nigeria too hot for me. The cultural shock was something I couldn't deal with and the expectations of me were more than I could ever offer.

My initial Nollywood experience was heartwarming. I was privileged to be cast in the same movie with Genevieve Nnaji and Chidi

Mokeme. I call it a privilege because they were already heavyweights in the industry. They knew their craft. They had the name and fame everyone craved in the industry. If you were a woman entering the movie industry in those days in Ghana or Nigeria, you could not fail to notice Genevieve and yearn to earn a bit of what she had made for herself. Surprisingly, however, Genevieve Nnaji turned out to be one of the exceptional women I have worked with or known in the movie industry. Her fame did not get into her head. She did not see herself up there and expect the rest of us minions to suck up to her. She was kind and considerate. She treated new entrants like me with the respect and dignity one would accord colleagues. She made me feel at home the same way Jackie Appiah made me feel when I began here in Ghana. Chidi was equally nice. He even hosted Kofi Adjorlolo and me in his house when we were in Nigeria.

Apart from Genevieve and a handful of actors, however, I do not have a very good account of the females in the industry. Most of them are predators. They make the lives of their colleagues miserable. Their superiority complex is obscene and they miss no opportunity to make others feel insignificant.

In Nollywood, for instance, there was an actress who was always weeping in movies. If you knew her only in movies, you would develop a soft spot for her meekness. In real life, however, she was a lioness. She would verbally abuse whoever crossed her path. She did not mind slapping her personal assistant or literally spitting on her. They found such behaviour as a normal part of the job. They commanded their reverence and whoever did not conform had to suffer their wrath.

I consider Nigerian producers and directors generally more efficient than their Ghanaian counterparts. They are able to make good use of their time and resources and get the best out of the cast. What often affected the smooth flow of proceedings were the egos of the big-name actors. There was a popular Nigerian actor who was shooting a movie and felt like visiting the washroom to pee. When she was offered a washroom, she rejected it even without inspecting it to see whether it met her so-called standard. She insisted on driving to her own home to use the washroom and return to the part of the city where we were shooting the movie. No amount of convincing worked. In the end, she had her way. We had to stop shooting until she returned.

Some of the big names sometimes prevailed on the directors to shoot their close-ups alone. These were scenes they said their lines with others, but without their partners in that scene showing. Sometimes, you needed their cues and reactions to bring out the best in your supporting role, but they would shoot theirs and leave and you had to act alone, reciting your lines and pretending the one you were talking to was next to you.

I later realised some of them were into drugs, which is not uncommon in the entertainment industry. They could get hyper even on set. There was this Nigerian actress who was always seen sipping something from an opaque bottle on set. I initially thought it was tea or some beverage, but it became common knowledge in the industry that it contained something stronger, something to enhance her performance.

I also thought the sexual advances were only from men until a popular but older Nollywood actress started to have issues with almost everything I did. For instance, she complained that whenever I met her on set, I refused to greet her. This charge surprised me because I had never gone on set without greeting the cast and crew. Unknown to me, she wanted to be greeted separately. If I walked into a meeting and greeted everyone together, she expected me to walk to her separately and greet her. This was not something I was used to. One of the directors called me aside after one of her outbursts and told me not to mind her.

"She is a lesbian and probably likes you," he told me.

I found her behaviour repulsive and did not ever get close enough for her to tell me whatever intentions she had towards me. As a producer, I am conscious of how I felt about these things as a young actor. I try not to subject others, especially young women, to the bullying I resented when I joined the industry. Despite the fact that some women have their own share of predatory behaviour, the interest of women will be better served if we had more women as producers and directors. It is part of the reason I press on with production in spite of the challenges. I feel if I quit as a producer, I will let many young women down. As far as I am concerned, a young man or woman does not need to do anything untoward to be given a chance. Their talents are enough. I guess the average female producer will be different from an average male producer in that regard.

In almost all the movies I have produced, I included new faces. In my latest movie titled *Tripping*, all the major actors are new entrants. I appear in only four scenes, but the lead actors have up to 150 scenes each. I try to be the opposite of what I dislike about the industry. Of course, I would get mad with a cast when he or she is not taking the work seriously, but one can be stern without being bullish or predatory.

As I grow in the industry, some of the motivations that used to drive me are giving way to new and more purposeful driving factors. I used to be fussy about awards, but I have come to see them as counterproductive. Awards are good, but they are someone's validation or opinion of you. If those people say you are the best actor this year and name someone else next year, it doesn't mean you cease to be the good actor that you are. I believe that if one allows awards to get into one's head, one will be enslaved by people's opinions. The danger here is that when the validations stop, you may think less of yourself and your capabilities.

After 17 years in the industry, I am looking up to a higher calling. There are many young women who look up to me and I don't want to let them down. As long as they are good enough to be given the platform, I will do my level best to offer them the stage. A person's talent should be enough. They should not be exploited if they want to rise. And, as a woman who has been in a position of vulnerability, my prayer is that I should be a different kind of producer. If a story is ever told of Yvonne Nelson Studios, it should be dominated by testimonies of great actors who had their breakthroughs without having to suffer the indignities that come with attaining fame.

CHAPTER FIFTEEN

An Entrepreneur

Children learn from their parents. The first impressions they form from watching their parents could influence what they do in the future. This is why I believe my mother's influence is partly responsible for my entrepreneurial drive.

I grew up watching my mother doing business. She was always counting money after the close of business each day. I didn't take an active part in her business, but I sometimes went around with her to her business contacts. I saw her buying and selling and making profit. She was a wholesaler of drinks and had a bar and provisions shop. On a few occasions, I took part in selling to customers. With this early encounter with commerce, doing business came to me naturally.

My mother's shop, Manovia, became my first shop. I renovated it and launched my clothing business, YN's Closet in 2008. That same year,

I added YN's Lace Wig to the clothing business. Acting presented me with those business ideas. The entertainment industry goes with fashion. Some people would dress a certain way because they see an actor or singer dress that way. What a favourite actor wears can influence the wardrobe of his or her followers. So, when I began to get compliments on my fashion sense, I decided to make a business out of it. I had to do something in line with my career and it would have been odd to venture into, for instance, the sale of car parts. I took an extra bag for shopping anytime I travelled abroad. When I had enough to stock a shop, YN's Closet was born.

After a year, I experienced growth and Manovia was too secluded for my flourishing business. I rented a shop in a part of Dansoman that was more visible and at a vantage point. The shop was at Dansoman First Stop, near the Dansoman campus of Central University College. The Methodist University was also in the area and the location had the kind of clientele base that would be interested in an Yvonne Nelson clothing line.

I was doing this business alongside acting. When I bought a house in Tema and had to leave Dansoman for good, it was difficult to keep the shop in Dansoman. I had employed someone to take care of the shop, but the distance was going to make it too difficult to monitor, so I closed the shop. My rent wasn't due so I handed the place to a friend who had expressed interest in continuing the business.

Moving to the Tema area put the business on hold, but the idea was still alive. When I returned to Accra two years later, I revisited it. I rented a shop at Bawaleshie near East Legon and revived YN's Closet. Behind that shop, I had a small office that served as the nerve centre of my production company. I ran that shop for five years and had to put it on hold again when I became pregnant. The pregnancy stagnated both my acting career and business because I was no longer travelling. I didn't have the opportunity to explore and shop for the business, so I finally gave the shop back to the landlord.

The second lady I hired to run the shop did not abandon me when the shop closed. She moved in with me and has been my God-sent nanny. Maanan Akoubor has been one of the biggest blessings of my life, and I dedicated my master's degree thesis to her. Without her, I couldn't have achieved what I did after I gave birth. I've been with her for close to six years and I cannot find the right words to express the profundity of my appreciation for her role in my life.

She has become like a sister, and we live like a family. She amazes me with the extent she is prepared to go for my daughter and me. I remember Ryn once fell sick and could hardly breathe. Maanan pulled the mucus from her nostrils with her mouth, something I would have found difficult to do as a mother. She did it without any hint that she'd gone the extra mile for my daughter. Maanan is one of the people who give me hope in humanity and the assurance that there are still good and dependable people around.

If YN's Closet stalled and remained as such to date, YN Productions didn't. I started YN Productions in 2010, the year I was banned and bullied by the Film Producers Association of Ghana. Beginning from the scratch was always going to be difficult, but when the motivation to succeed was far greater than just making money, I put in my all. I had learned quickly and was prepared to take on the world. That didn't go without opposition.

I paid the price with the first movie I produced, *The Price*. Someone broke into the editor's suite and stole the hard drives and other storage devices. I lost everything. Determined to continue, I reassembled the cast and begged them to reshoot. Due to budgetary constraints and the wane in enthusiasm, the reshoot didn't come out the way I had expected, but it had to be done. I had taken money from an executive producer to fund that movie and could not have gone back to tell him that I lost the project. The funder, who also owned Media GH, organisers of the Ghana Meet Naija annual musical concert, kept faith with me in those early years. Media GH funded my next two movies, Single and Married, and House of Gold. That company owned the right to my first three movies, which were well received. After the third attempt, I decided it was time to find my own money for my productions.

The first output of that initiative was a sequel to Single and Married, which was *Single, Married* and *Complicated*. I followed that up with If Tomorrow Never Comes, a movie based on the true story of a boy with cerebral abnormalities. My movies have been well-received in Ghana and in Nigeria. At one point, they were leading in popularity in the cinemas of the two countries. My next production was the series Heels and Sneakers, which I had to pause because I got pregnant in the third season.

Bouncing back after pregnancy and childbirth was dogged by difficulty and uncertainty. I had been away for a while and had to restart as an actor and a producer. I was unsure how movie lovers were going to receive me. I had starred as the lead actor in a number of the movies I produced. Childbirth changed my looks and affected my confidence. But I was not going to allow uncertainty and self-doubt to hold me down further. Being a woman comes with a price. I had already lost a lot. If I waited further, the right time might never come.

I confronted my fears and produced Sin City. That movie blew me away. It was as if movie patrons had been starved of my production for too long, so they came in droves. Sin City did better than any other movie I had produced. I soon learnt that if your patrons have faith in you, they will stick with you. I filled about 10 cinema halls the night the movie premiered.

My most successful movie, however, has been The Men We Love. When that movie premiered, I said to myself that the movie industry wasn't dead. What people wanted were good movies. My next movie was Fifty Fifty. The premiering coincided with torrential rainfall in Accra, but moviegoers braved the rains and we managed to fill up to eight halls on the night.

So far, YN Productions has produced 14 movies. They are: (1) The Price (2) Single and Married (3) Single, Married and Complicated (4) House of Gold (5) If Tomorrow Never Comes (6) Sin City (7) Heals and Sneakers—Seasons 1-3 (8) Fix Us (9) The Men We Love (10) Fifty Fifty (11) Summer (12) Kotoka (13) Tripping (14) Waiting for Ryn, a documentary series.

As a producer, I have benefited immensely from the support of great friends in the industry. Of special mention is Majid Michel. He is one of the closest and most supportive friends I have in the industry. I do better with him and he has been one of the most outstanding backbones of YN Productions.

If movie production is directly in line with what I do, there is a business I discovered in 2019 that is turning out to be something I'm not only passionate about but also have a sentimental attachment to. It began when I was looking for a school where I could be comfortable leaving my daughter. I needed a school where I wouldn't have to worry about what happened to her. The school I sent her to did not give me that assurance. She had returned from school one day with a bruise on her skin. When I asked, the school told me someone had opened the door and it accidentally hit her. No one had told me about it, an attitude I least expected from that calibre of school.

In 2019, I registered Just Like Mama Day Care. I spent considerable time researching and learning to ensure that the school would take off without any hitches. I spoke to school consultants, principals and other experts on what I needed to have in a good school. I researched the potential challenges and how to surmount them. I started to research and learn on my own as I began to set up classrooms and took care of the artwork.

I wanted to open it in 2020, but the Covid-19 pandemic turned the world upside down and stalled my plans. The school started in January 2021, and when I entered the school on the first day and heard a baby cry, I couldn't believe that a school I had set up was being patronised. It was surreal, and for a moment, I felt like joining the baby to cry. The school started with a creche, lower and upper nursery, and kindergartens 1 and 2. We are in our second year and we already have 50 amazing children.

Due to my background as an entertainer, I harboured doubts about the readiness of parents to bring their children to the school. Some people believe everything they hear about celebrities. For those of us into acting, a movie role can take the place of your personality. There are people who see you play a thief in a movie and think you're a thief. Being arrogant in Princess Tyra stayed with the Yvonne Nelson name for a long time. For the first time, however, I am beginning to learn something new. It taught me that the faith in my brand is bigger than I had imagined. The feedback from parents who have seen great improvements in their children keeps pushing me to do more.

Some parents have already started asking what is next for their children after Kindergarten 2. They are eager to have a continuation for their children in a clean and conducive environment, a school where their children will be pushed to the limits of their abilities as we do at Just Like Mama Day Care.

Whatever I have set up as an entrepreneur may be considered a business, but with the school, I'm beginning to see a calling. The motivation is greater than any financial gain. It is a unique opportunity to shape minds and impact generations. I have ranted enough about what is wrong with our educational system. I find this the greatest challenge of my life, a challenge to create something that is different from grammar or memory and recall. It is a call to make a mark. And it is a call to which I am responding with all the dedication and devotion I can muster.

Movies produced by YN Productions

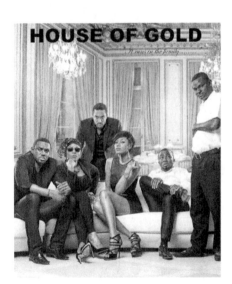

Scenes at the premiere of my movies

174

CHAPTER SIXTEEN

Celebrity Bubble and The Ring I Accepted with Tears

In 2019, one of my followers on Instagram decided to troll me. Of all the problems in this world, his was that I had repeated the same slippers too many times in the photos I shared on that social media platform. I was unconscious of the repetition, but he had the time and presence of mind to track the different occasions I had won the same slippers and taken photos with them. I probably had worn them on more outings than he thought because I surely did not take a photograph anytime I wore those slippers. And if I took photographs each time, I definitely could not post all of them on Instagram. So my "offence" was obviously graver than he thought. My response to him sent news websites and entertainment blogs into a frenzy. It even featured in entertainment news on radio and television.

"Most of the 'flyyyy' life you see celebs putting out there isn't real," I told him. "Peeps got to keep up! Yea, it's kind of part of the job, but it's too much work for me. I'm being myself here. For those living on Jupiter, I'm sorry. Down here on earth where I live, I can wear my Hermes slippers a million times!"

Even before I responded to the troll, some had taken the battle personally. A Nigerian lady particularly took on the fight and put the cyberbully where he belonged. Of course, there would always be those who latch onto the silliest attacks and make you feel less of yourself, but I had long gone past the stage where I could be put down by such comments. I didn't feel I owed anybody an explanation for repeating my wardrobe. I would have cared and brooded over that comment a few years earlier. I wouldn't have had the courage to repeat the same outfit many times and certainly would have felt too embarrassed to defend it. At the time this attacker went low against me, however, I had outgrown the curse of celebrity lifestyle and was on my way to maturity. It came at a time when my convictions mattered more to me than courting the fleeting buzz of public approval. It was a time I cared little about meeting the public's expectation of a celebrity, a name I started hearing of myself when I shot into the movie industry.

There is no consensus on who earns the right to be called a celebrity. Some people think one must command a certain amount of following and be celebrated for an outstanding skill, mostly in entertainment or sport, to be called a celebrity. Others think being famous in your community cannot make you a celebrity. To them, you must attain some national and, in some instances, international recognition to be called a celebrity. There are those who are called celebrities, and there are those who call themselves celebrities. It appears, however, that the people out there are the custodians who confer that hallowed, sometimes, hollow title, which some are prepared to kill for. It is the public and individuals who determine who their celebrity is. An international pop star will mean nothing to someone in a community that has never heard about the pop star. That person may, however, idolize a community singer and see him or her as a celebrity.

The meaning of celebrity used to be clearer until the advent of social media. It used to denote and connote the same thing. It was associated with fame. It was associated with popularity, being known and celebrated for something positive. To some, it came as an acquired status. They worked and excelled in one craft or the other and earned the right to be described as such. To others, being a celebrity was an ascribed status, one that was thrust upon them by virtue of their birth or lineage. In whatever way one acquired one's celebrity status, there were some parameters with which celebrities were measured, even if those parametres were not strictly defined.

These days, however, it's much easier to be a celebrity. You don't have to do much. A thriving social media account and a decent amount of following—amassed through any means possible—bestows a celebrity status on the account holder and gives him or her access to the red carpet. I am not envious or worried about the invasion, delusion and desecration of the celebrity space. The universe is big enough to contain everyone. However, I still habour the fear of sounding presumptuous in calling myself a celebrity, long after I started to be described as such by the media, my followers and people in my social circles. I am careful not to live another day in the celebrity bubble because it is the opium that can cloud one's sense of reasoning and plant a visible tower of crowd-pleasing mindset. Living in that bubble places public opinion above common sense and pragmatism. It is more about faking, and I believe life is easier when one is real.

Being a celebrity comes with a burden. Those who are unable to manage it are ruled and eventually ruined by it. The expectation of a celebrity is aptly described in these lines in Michael Jackson's Will You Be There? track:

Everyone's taking control of me
Seems that the world's got a role for me
I'm so confused...

If you are a celebrity, everyone would want to take control of you and prescribe a role for you. You are likely to be confused. You may not know exactly what you want because those casting you in the roles of their non-existent fantasy movies may have no clue either. It is showbiz, the business of showing and make-believe. It is the business of keeping appearances—physical appearance and emotional appearance. A celebrity's physical appearance requires that you sometimes live beyond your means and invest in enterprises that yield no returns. It means borrowing to change your car every year or striving to wear designer clothes that drain your earnings and drown you in debt if your earnings don't match the appearance you're expected to keep. If

178

you cannot pull the breaks, you may engage in fraudulent deals or open your legs to those who have the money to fund your vanity. These are realities in the industry I found myself in. This side of the celebrity world is not often captured by the same cameras that paint the rosy pictures of glamour and glitz.

In terms of emotional appearance, the celebrity is expected to show positivity and be cheerful and happy. You're to let the world believe you're on cloud nine even when you're at the lowest ebb of gloom. Your tears are your fears, for they show a weakness that mustn't be associated with you. Clothing and make-up can cover physical blemishes, but they cannot make up for the gaping deficit between one's true emotional state and the appearance they must put up in public. Many celebrities, therefore, resort to drugs to manage their emotional imbalances. For many, that is the only way to stay afloat in the turbulent waters of showbiz. It is an inescapable trap that keeps you enslaved to the dictates of public opinion and makes you cringe at the words of people who have no business having certain expectations of you. There was a time in my career that I lived for the cameras.

Growing up, I didn't prepare for the trappings of fame or public life. I had no clue that someone else would celebrate me when my own father disowned me, and my mother and siblings were obviously not proud of my poor academic performance. So, I couldn't have anticipated stardom and prepared for it. My luck, however, was that my background anchored me and kept me on the shores of sanity when there was the temptation to go haywire. I had a point to prove to my family. I had to show that I wasn't useless after all. I needed to prove that I was somebody. It was the reason I took investment seriously when I started earning money. Before I even thought of buying my first house, I had helped to renovate my mother's house in Dansoman. We replaced the louvres with sliding windows because times were changing. We tiled the floors, changed the ceiling and painted the house. When it was done, I chose my late grandmother's room. It was in this room that I used to hold her long breasts, the breasts I nicknamed "bombo" when I was a child. The fact that she had died did not scare me. Some fear living in the rooms of a deceased person. My bed was where hers had been, and I thought I would live there for a long time. I had borne about 70% of the cost of the renovation and felt profoundly proud that I was a major contributor to the family.

My mother was proud of me, but, as is usual of her, she wouldn't say much about it. However, instead of telling, she showed it later. It showed in the decision she wanted to take. She wanted to will that house to me, perhaps, because of the role I had played in the make-over of the old version of it. That decision didn't sit well with me. I didn't think I needed it. And even if I did, that wouldn't be fair to my two siblings. I would be happy to rent it out and share the proceeds with them instead of taking it all alone.

I had no problem living in my mother's house even at a time I was a household name, but others did. A female friend I met in the movie industry was not tired of reminding me that I needed to rent my own apartment and move from my mother's house. Her words had an effect on me, but I didn't act on them. I knew where I lived was just a phase of life, but I had to move at my own pace. When the time was ripe, I did not rent as she had suggested. I moved into my own house. When I was moving to my second house, the same lady who had pestered me to rent a place wanted me to rent out my first house to her.

I cannot pretend that I haven't been affected by the pressures of the celebrity lifestyle. There was a time I bought bags I didn't need. I had to show off. My first car was a necessity and I didn't mind the make or model. All I needed was something to help move my hustle. My second and third were more than that. I was conscious of the choices I was making and the need to keep my place in the industry. What car which celebrity drove was as important as which role one played in a movie. There were times I wore clothes to impress. What others thought of me preceded everything else in my decision on what hairpiece to invest in.

My Damascus moment, however, came before I turned 30, so I can say I burst my celebrity bubble less than a decade into my career. It happened when I was turning 29. It suddenly dawned on me that I would soon be 30, and that I would begin my journey into old age sooner than I had imagined.

At 29, I wasn't the happiest of ladies you could find. On the outside, things were moving on well, but they didn't translate into internal joy and peace of mind. For instance, I was dating a man I didn't love, a man who was making marriage plans while I was planning how to opt

181

out without hurting him too much. On my 29th birthday, he took me to Venice, the city of love and romance. I knew he was going to pop the question, and it scared the hell out of me. The night before my birthday, I called my mother and wept uncontrollably on the phone. I could smell the proposal the following night after dinner, and I wasn't prepared for it. The response I was about to give would come from my mouth but had no place in my heart. My mother was confused. The man checked all the boxes of a decent and modern-day gentleman, the kind of man every sane woman would gravitate toward when she thinks of settling down. He appeared to be at the stage of his life where he needed to settle down. He had a blistering career. He owned a beach house in London.

But love works differently. It doesn't care about society's standards. It has its own standards. The standards of love may fail the test of logic, but that's love. It works in its own way. Some say love is a decision and not a feeling, but how you feel about someone sometimes determines the decision you make about them. Either way, there is some element of feeling that cannot be completely dismissed.

Besides, the demands of marriage far exceed the expectations of love. Marriage is deeper than love. Even if I had giant butterflies fluttering inside me, I knew a time would come in the marriage when they would cease to exist. It is what remains when love dies that should guide one's decision to marry a particular person. In my case, I didn't see the strong presence of either ingredient—the ingredients of the head and that of the heart. I had hoped that I would warm my way into the relationship

182

as time went on, but the more we travelled, the more I felt I didn't belong in that journey. And as the opportunity to opt out as harmlessly as possible became more and more elusive, he was complicating things by going ahead to propose marriage to me.

On that fateful night, we had a romantic dinner after a boat ride earlier in the day. When I opened the dessert bowl after the dinner, some vapour-like cloud hovered briefly over the plate before clearing to expose the ring. He proposed to me with his mother's ring. That's how seriously he took it. It meant so much to him and nothing to me. My preoccupation was how to not ruin his night.

"Will you marry me?" he asked.

I nodded.

A witness to that romantic proposal in Venice might include in his or her narrative that the bride-to-be was too overwhelmed with emotions to speak, so she nodded. Of course, as a woman whose claim to fame was acting, adding colour to the scene came to me as second nature. It had to look good for the cameras and to the eyes that might have been envying me, instead of pitying him. After the proposal and my birthday, we flew back to London, and when I was still weighing my options, he made things easier. His attitude provided a parachute for me to jump out and land safely before the plane of our relationship got into complicated altitudes.

183

This man always wanted us to eat out, and whenever he was going to work, he preferred that I held on to the irresistible demands of my hunger pangs until he returned. I remember he once left two fingers of banana as what I should eat so that we go out after about 3 p.m. when he returned. This was not the treatment someone like me who worshipped food would tolerate. After the proposal, while I was deciding how to execute my plan after my return to Ghana, he pushed the nuclear code too early.

A female friend had visited me while he was away at work. Esi and I were in the house when he returned. He was rude to her, taking the television remote disapprovingly from her and changing the channel. When Esi failed to get his memo, he called me aside and gave what sounded like a stern instruction. He had expected Esi to leave as soon as he entered the house. His unwholesome attitude had failed to get Esi out so he wanted me to tell her to leave right away.

I left with Esi and returned his ring to him through DHL.

After that, the thought of turning 30 and growing old assailed me. That was when I began to pay attention to the things that mattered most in life. I was beginning to think more about adding value to myself and perfecting my trade. My liberation came when I started to care less about what people said, the expectation of society of me and how I ought to respond to the demands of fame. I was beginning to think of how to give meaning to my life. It came with its own doubts and, sometimes, confusion. But that turning point before thirty proved pivotal in my life. It defined the other major decisions I made afterward, such as setting up a school and paying more attention to my businesses.

After having Ryn, I decided to go back to school. In 2018, I went to the Ghana Institute of Management and Public Administration (GIMPA) to pursue a Master's in International Relations and Diplomacy. I entertained the idea of venturing into politics or governance after the overwhelming endorsements and suggestions that came my way in the wake of the #DumsorMustStop protest. If an opportunity ever presented itself, I didn't want to grab it blindly and cluelessly. I had to be prepared. I needed to have something to offer beyond my fame in the entertainment industry. I needed to know how the world spun and be familiar with the interplay of power and the role of an individual like me in it.

Going back to school also served as a welcome distraction from postpartum depression that reared its head menacingly after I had my child. Her father was in London, and I did not have the companionship and emotional support I needed. It didn't help that I saw him on social media with younger women. Ours wasn't a relationship that endured. It wasn't fair to expect him to be tethered to someone with whom he had no future. In my mind, he was free to be with whomever he wanted to be with, but my heart couldn't be at peace with the reasoning of my mind. I had lost business opportunities and acting roles because of pregnancy and childbirth. I had lost my shape and was not sure when I would recover enough to be on set, to be Yvonne Nelson again. While I brooded over this, the man who had put me in that state was enjoying life as if nothing had happened. It was tough. School, therefore, gave me something to think about, but it was not easy either.

Ryn wanted fresh breastmilk always. When I pumped breastmilk into a feeding bottle for her, she refused it. She wanted it fresh from the source, perhaps, because it gave her the opportunity to cuddle and suck the love that came with the nutritious milk. Compelling her to adapt to the new formula pained me. My attention was always torn between lectures and my pretty little angel at home. There were times I asked why I got myself into this situation, but it was worth it. I sometimes spent the whole day on campus and would return home after 7 p.m. The joy of holding another being that depended wholly on me was therapeutic but challenging.

Until that bundle of joy came into my life, I used to think more about myself and what I could do with my life. It is now more about her. Knowing that I have a responsibility toward her— a duty of care, and a charge to make her world better than mine, keeps me going. It has added another layer of maturity that I was forced to embrace before I turned 32. I'm heading towards 40 and motherhood has taught me an awful lot that nothing in the world could have taught me.

CHAPTER SEVENTEEN

The Prize and Price of Motherhood

It was in a friend's bathroom in March 2017 that I discovered I was pregnant. I had attended her birthday party the day before and slept over. The following morning, I had a strong urge to have a pregnancy test, having missed my period. So, I bought the test kit and went to the bathroom. And that was when it dawned on me that my life was about to change in a significant way.

I had spent February that year in London with Jamie. It was at the peak of our relationship, and we had special moments together, including on Valentine's Day. In March, I was back in Ghana, and when I missed my period, I knew something was brewing inside me. (I remember the doctor gave me November 12 as my due date for delivery. I was excited because that was my birthday, but Ryn came two weeks earlier). The result of the test was a confirmation of what I thought it was. It was also a validation that I was capable of conceiving, something I had had reason to doubt.

My desire to have children started when I turned 29. By my 30th birthday, it almost became desperation. I remember a particular spot in my bedroom at Redrow Estates, where I would lie down and pray to God for a child. I had not been told anywhere that I was incapable of conceiving, but self-doubt and the reality that not every woman is able to have her own child heightened my anxiety. In my case, the history of the abortion years ago and its complications stoked my fear and dimmed my odds whenever the thought of having my own children came up. Getting pregnant was, therefore, an answer to my intense prayer. It was a miracle, for the whole process of having a human being form from a tiny drop of semen and grow inside you is a miracle. I felt privileged and received it with gladness.

Jamie was equally happy that I was pregnant for him. I had always wanted to have children, but meeting him settled any reservation about anything to the contrary. His relationship with his children was great. It convinced me that should I want a father figure for my child, then this was the ideal man. That preoccupation did not consider the possibility that things could go wrong. He lived in London and I lived in Ghana, but the possibility of the relationship going sour and our children being left stranded did not cross my mind. Things seemed too perfect to ever go wrong. It remained so until I became pregnant.

Jamie said we should keep the news to ourselves until after three months. I understood him and did just that. So, it was after the third month that I broke the news to my mother. I set up the camera and announced it to her. I wanted to have memories of her reaction so I set up the camera without letting her know. She was happy for me, but that happiness soon dissipated and left in its wake a palpable worry. She was happy that I was pregnant and would bring forth a child, but her worry stemmed from the fact that I was not married. She did not hide that worry. She expressed it, but I was determned that nothing in that regard would dim my joy. I had outgrown those concerns, so I told her that I was okay with whatever was happening in my life. I was in control, with or without a husband.

The next few weeks into my second trimester were frantic moments for me. It was as though I was going about my daily outdoor chores until an unannounced downpour started, forcing me to halt and get indoors. I couldn't get inside with many things hanging in the rain. They needed to be carried inside. I knew my career was going to be interrupted. Just how long that would be, I could not say. I was not going to be featured in other people's movies for a long time to come. I could not feature in my own movies and would certainly not be able to produce them. My clothing business was going to suffer because I could not supervise or travel to replenish the depleting stock as was my custom.

When I discovered that I was pregnant, I was shooting Heels and Sneakers. I had to shoot as many episodes as possible before my abdomen bulged. In the latter days of the shooting, the cast and crew who paid attention would have suspected that all was not well with me. Though my abdomen did not give any clue, I spat a lot. And whoever had been with me for long or known me would wonder what was happening to me.

I didn't want the news of my pregnancy and its attendant reactions and attacks to complicate the already complex life I was confronting. The decision was therefore to keep it out of public eyes and ears and mouths. Only a few trusted friends knew I was pregnant. To quell the public gossip, I subjected myself to solitary confinement in my home. If I needed to shop for groceries, I sent for them. I cancelled all appointments and did not accept new ones. The only place I drove to was my mother's house in Dansoman, and I was careful that nothing would blow my cover, literally.

Part of the reason I frequented my mother's place was to placate my weird cravings. I couldn't taste pepper when I became pregnant, but that didn't stop me from craving for peppery foods. I remember I would ask my mother to prepare gari with pepper and crabs, which I savoured with satisfaction. I also craved warm milk. At times, that was all I needed. I would warm the milk, and drink it. The next moment, I would fall asleep.

The loneliness was, perhaps, part of the reason I suffered so much during my pregnancy. Jamie visited in the first trimester of my pregnancy and did not return until a few days before my delivery date.

The emotional support and love I needed most in this period were missing. But that was not all. I was also going through pain. I had read the email from Jamie's ex-wife and knew our relationship had no future. Knowing that was one thing, and accepting the reality was another. So, even though I knew that our beautiful and almost perfect relationship had hit a hard and impenetrable rock, it was still difficult to ignore any social media post he made with another woman. With my hormones all over the place and the least issue triggering depression, I felt like he had put my life and my world on hold and did not even care about it. He could have gone out with those ladies, but if he wasn't doing that to spite me, he would have kept the outings from social media, I thought. Did he know what I was going through? Did he care about posting a black lady he had taken to the restaurant he once told me was his favourite? His choice of women was black and if he took a black lady to his choicest restaurant and posted about it, I didn't need any confirmation from him that they were dating. Did he care about the impact of that on me? I answered all these questions negatively, and those answers pushed a dagger into my heart.

One of the worst moments during my pregnancy came through a phone call from Nigeria. I had an endorsement deal with Glo, and the call came from there. I remember a woman called me to shoot an ad and I came clean with her that I was pregnant. I explained that I would deliver in three or four months and we could continue with everything. Her response was: "The dynamics will change." I did not have the opportunity to deliver and continue with the deal. Shortly after that, my contract with Glo was not renewed, and I knew it was down to the pregnancy. That broke me. But I had to fight on and live for the precious being inside me.

Though it was my first pregnancy, I did not have a lot of physical complications. It was more of the emotional distress. The absence of companionship made the burden heavier. I attended the antenatal clinic alone and had to take extraordinary measures to ensure that news of my pregnancy did not leak. At the hospital, my folder did not have my name. I went by the name Regina Van Helvet. I remember there were times I had to be prompted by a nurse that I was the one being called because I forgot the pseudonym I had chosen for myself. When my baby was finally born, her cot did not have my name. It was Regina Van Helvet. I watched it and smiled, momentarily forgetting the drama that heralded the arrival of that little angel.

My water broke on October 29, 2017. It was at about 5 a.m. in the 38th week of my pregnancy. It was a Sunday morning when I felt the gush of water down my thighs. I immediately knew I had to get to the hospital. I had learnt from my antenatal sessions and my own research (reading and watching YouTube videos) about what to expect. I had downloaded apps that showed the development of the baby at the various stages of the pregnancy and what to expect. I was always on top of issues. Nothing took me by surprise, so when the water broke, I knew the moment had arrived, and I needed to get to the hospital as soon as possible.

Jamie had been back a few days earlier and was with me, but I couldn't trust him to drive me. Ghana and Britain drive on different sides of the road and whoever switches without enough practice is likely to cause havoc. The last time Jamie had tried driving in Ghana, he almost killed himself. In a state that required utmost care in order to get to the hospital alive, therefore, I could not trust him to transport me.

The first person who came to mind was Sammy Forson, a broadcast journalist who lived in the area. When I called him, however, he did not answer. I then called Nii, another friend who lived around. He, too, did not answer his phone. In that mode of controlled panic, I was running out of options until I remembered a neighbour, Johnson Kotey, whom I had given my dog to. I had a dog, but the demands of pregnancy, allergies and other related issues did not permit me to give the dog the needed care so I gave her out.

Mr. Kotey was getting ready for church when my call came. He responded quickly and was at my gate the next moment. With him in the driving seat and Jamie and I behind, we headed for the Lister Hospital and Fertility Centre at Airport Hills. It was a 9-kilometre journey that lasted longer than the 20 minutes it normally would require to cover that distance. At the time, the road from my house to School Junction and to Adjiringanor was not tarred. This meant that the driver had to exercise utmost caution in order not to worsen my delicate situation. Speed was of the essence, but arriving safely was more important. When we got to the Underbridge at East Legon, however, things changed.

193

The baby's head was visible through my vulva, when we were still about two kilometres away from the hospital. The road from Underbridge to the hospital was tarred and would not take us long to get there, but it was almost too late. My baby's head was already showing, and the pain was something I had never felt before, not even during my near-death abortion experience. I had read that the stage I was in was called crowning, but nothing had prepared me for the pain that came with it. It was as if a million people were holding my vagina and trying to forcibly open it to allow the baby out. In order not to hurt the baby, I could not sit. I held the hand grab of the vehicle tightly and suspended between my seat and the driver's seat.

When the driver turned and saw the baby's head popping out of my vagina, he shouted, "Oh my God! Oh my God!"

"Drive!" I barked back at him. And he literally flew like a formula one driver.

Jamie had, by now, learnt to mind his business or rather keep his worries and encouragements to himself. He was the one who bore the brunt of my fire that morning. When the pain intensified and he tried to comfort me, I screamed at him to shut up, for he had no idea what I was going through. He appeared to forget this instruction often and instinctively offered words of comfort, but nothing made sense in that moment of excruciating pain.

When we finally arrived at the hospital, I was given a wheelchair. I thought a stretcher would have been ideal for my situation. The baby's head was already coming out so I could not sit properly or even close my legs in the wheelchair. I however managed to hang in there in a way that would not cause any harm to my baby. When I got onto the delivery bed, I was asked to push. I had felt the urge to push while in the car, but the confusion of not wanting the baby to come out in the car and not knowing exactly how to push had put that urge on hold. I still could not tell whether I was pushing the right way, but the midwife leading the team that delivered me suggested a cut. She produced a pair of scissors and cut the opening to my vagina. Shortly afterwards, my baby slipped out effortlessly.

When Ryn was handed to me, I quickly instructed them to take her away. I wanted to hold her forever, but considering the torturous journey, I wasn't sure if she arrived with all the safety boxes ticked. I, therefore, wanted them to be sure she was absolutely fine before returning her to me. After all, I would spend the rest of my life with her and I could cuddle her as much as I wanted. After cleaning her, the nurses brought her back to me. She was healthy and unscathed except for the few days after the delivery when we noticed that her eyes were yellowing and returned her to the hospital. She was diagnosed with and treated for jaundice.

The joy of seeing and holding Ryn in my hospital bed numbed any pain that still lingered. It erased the loneliness and stress I suffered during the pregnancy. It placed a weight of responsibility that would forever alter my worldview and dictate my actions and choices. Since she came, I have been more careful and more purposeful about life. She is an anchor of stability in my life, a guardrail against carelessness. She is a constant awakener of my sense of awareness that I no longer live for myself only. I am more careful with every step I take. I have a responsibility to guide her through the unpredictable maze of life until she is old enough to be on her own. I dread the consequences of leaving her in the middle of nowhere, making her vulnerable to the merciless vagaries of human actions.

She was my comfort when the custodians of morality descended on me with harsh judgment and condemnation. I posted a magazine cover of my pregnancy on November 12, 2017, my birthday. I had managed to keep it out of the gossip mill and out of the prying eyes of bloggers. However, about 30 minutes after my delivery, the news was already out that I had a baby. If I had managed to keep my pregnancy a secret, I lost control of the environment when I got to the hospital on the day of my delivery. I was not in control of the narrative and could definitely not have stopped any health worker from texting a friend or colleague that Yvonne Nelson had delivered a baby girl.

So, while I was battling with my own postpartum, the merciless judges in the court of public opinion had their way and their say. To them, I was a role model to many young women and the fact that I had given birth without being married sent the wrong signal. I had broken a moral code and could influence those who looked up to me.

These and others are the pressures that often force young women to terminate pregnancies when they are not prepared to face the world. Having suffered it and almost lost my life, it is not something anyone takes lightly. When I had my baby, I would not say I didn't care about the attacks. I was, however, mature enough to stand them. Besides, I had to be strong for myself and my child. I had to live to see her grow. I had to live to teach her to be a woman of valour. I want to teach her to be a woman who will respect other people no matter their creed, race or status in society. I want her to be that woman who will believe in herself and her convictions.

My pregnancy was a secret, but I went to the studio of Bob Pixel for a photo shoot

I had a photo shoot at Aburi Botanical Garden

Satisfying my weird cravings in Dansoman

Pregnant and supervising the construction of my house

"The loneliness was, perhaps, part of the reason I suffered so much during my pregnancy. Jamie visited in the first trimester of my pregnancy and did not return until a few days before my delivery date..."

In this photo: Jamie's hand on me during labour

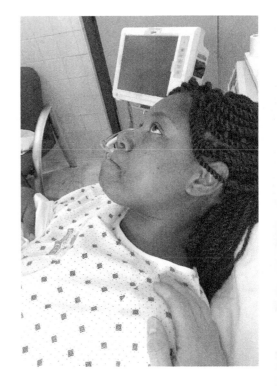

Finally, Ryn arrived and the joy dispelled memories of the pain I had felt.

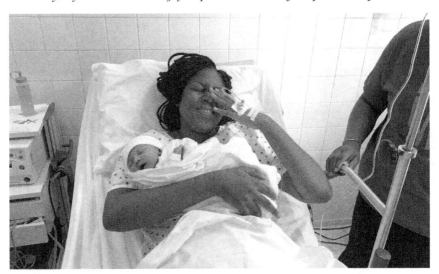

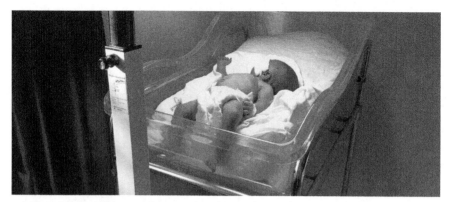

After delivery, Ryn was diagnosed with jaundice and was treated

With Ryn when she was about three months old

Ryn loves being carried in an African cloth

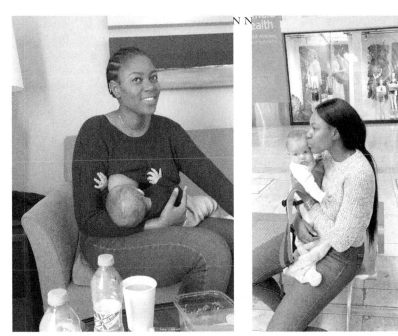

I visited London when Ryn was five months old. We went to see other members of her father's family.

I granted the BBC an interview on my visit to London after delivery.

With Ryn in Dubai for my 36th birthday

With Ryn in my bedroom in Ghana

Former President Kufuor was happy to see Ryn and me. It was my next visit to him after we last spoke about Peter Ala Adjetey.

With Former President Kufuor when I went to see him about Peter Ala Adjetey

After having Ryn, I decided to go back to school. In 2018, I went to the Ghana Institute of Management and Public Administration (GIMPA) to pursue a Master's in International Relations and Diplomacy. I entertained the idea of venturing into politics or governance after the overwhelming endorsements and suggestions that came my way in the wake of the #DumsorMustStop protest. If an opportunity ever presented itself, I didn't want to grab it blindly and cluelessly.

LIKE MAMA • DAY CARE

PLaY LeArn gRow

Est. 2019

Just Like Mama Day Care is more than just a business. I see it as a calling.

BERS 1 one to 100 one hundred

6 7 8 eight 9 10 ten

19 20 twenty

PART THREE

THE SEARCH FOR MY FATHER

CHAPTER EIGHTEEN

A Visit to Mr. Nelson

For many children, a father is a father. There are no complications to that simple biological fact. The few that have exceptions may be familiar with the words "step", "foster" or "adopted" preceding their fathers. Even with that, as they grow, they receive clues about who their real fathers are or were. They get full briefings about the circumstances of their birth. Such people, in many instances, are given the back stories and disclosures that bring closure to any lingering doubts about their identities.

In my case, I was neither an adopted nor stepchild as far as my father was concerned, and there was nothing to show he was my biological father. I was made to believe that Mr. Nelson didn't like me. He, on the other hand, had given me enough reason to doubt his paternity of me. He treated me like an unwholesome and unwelcome visitor. The older I grew, the more I resented him. When I asked my mother, I heard the same stories she told me since my primary school teacher called Eugene Nelson and me and asked whether we shared a father.

I had vowed to keep probing and asking until I discovered the truth, but the more I discovered, the more I felt as though I had been handed the script of a suspense-laden family drama with a wild and endless plot. It is a story that reaches the climax and stays there because the resolution dissipates just as you feel you have everything under your grasp. At a point, I felt wrapping my head around the truth was as impossible as wrapping my hands around the trunk of an elephant. My anxiety was mainly because I knew someone who knew the truth, and that truth was within my reach. It felt like an itch in the part of my body I could never reach and scratch, but I had vowed not to give up. It was the reason I kept my eyes on the ball, not wandering too far from the vexed subject.

I did not take "no answer" for an answer. I kept going back to the subject, taking advantage of incidents, events and clues and going back to the one and only source that knew the whole truth—my mother. I went to the same source I felt was keeping the truth away from me until I discovered I could go farther than what she told me. I was determined to find an answer because the woman who was denying me the answer had found answers to her own paternity after she became a mother of three children.

My mother had grown up not knowing her father. Or rather, she knew the wrong father. She bore the surname Glover-Addy. She told

208

me how hellish life was in the house of Mr. Glover-Addy. The man's wife, she told me, couldn't stand her. She felt it was beyond the usual tale of a fractured relationship between a stepmother and a stepchild. The house did not lack substance, but the size of the bread the woman served her was enough communication that the intention was to starve, and not to feed her.

Such treatment was, perhaps, part of the reason a semblance of affection swept her off her feet and expedited her decision to get married as a teenager. She left the home of the Glover-Addys at age 19 to live with the father of my siblings, but she carried the scars of the treatment she was subjected to for a long time. She still regrets that early marriage, which she says robbed her of education and other dreams. If finding her feet in business and chalking some modest successes in different aspects of her life made her discard the burden of mistreatment in Mr. Glover-Addy's house, there's one thing she still bears—the name Glover-Addy.

Many years later, however, she would discover that the man she had thought was her father had no biological relationship with her. I still remember when she took me to the house of the man I later found to be her real father. She had driven me to a house around Nima, a suburb of Accra, and spent a long time in the house. She left me in the car, and I suspected she didn't want me to know what was ensuing in the house. When she finally remerged, she was with a light-complexioned man whom I would later know as Edward Mahjoub. That man was her brother. I have seen the photos of their father, Mr. Mahjoub, but I didn't meet him until he passed.

Their father, Mr. Mahjoub, was of Ghanaian and Lebanese parentage, and that explained my mother's light complexion. My mother is an exceptionally intelligent woman, so growing up with such a complexion when her mother and Glover-Addy were dark must have raised questions. Whatever her doubts were, she cleared them later in life. I'm unable to tell whether being kept in the dark for so long affected her relationship with her mother—my grandmother—but I know their relationship was not in the best of shapes.

Under these circumstances, the only grandparent I knew was my grandmother, my mother's mother. I should have known four grandparents, the mothers and fathers of my father and mother, but that was not what I grew up with. Mr. Nelson, I was convinced, did not want to see me, so introducing me to his parents was out of the question. As a child, I also vowed never to go to his house. I didn't care who his parents were. That also meant I had a limited family tree and heritage.

When people ask about my hometown, I mention Ajumako Bisease in the Central Region. Other times, I say Takoradi, for my grandmother said she hailed from Ajumako Bisease but grew up in Effiakuma in Takoradi in the Western Region of Ghana. I was born at the Korle-Bu Teaching Hospital and grew up in Dansoman. When they ask about my ethnicity, I say I'm half-Fante and half-something else. I don't know where the other half comes from. The desire to know that welled up strongly in me as I made what would become my last visit to Mr. Nelson's house. It was my first visit since I became an adult.

It was in 2016, shortly before I met my daughter's father. I had just turned 31, and our meeting was in December of that year. Looking back, it seems there was something divine about the whole episode. At the time, I was filming Heels and Sneakers, and one of my cast members who was fasting asked me to join him. I obliged and was supposed to fast for a week or so. Fasting is the icing on my spiritual cake. I love food and smell food all the time whenever I fast. It seems God knows this and pays serious attention to my prayers whenever I fast. One of the issues I prayed about while fasting with my cast member was the unresolved puzzle about my father.

In the course of the fast, one of Mr. Nelson's children told me he was sick. The person told me things were not looking good, and I felt I had to go and see the old man. I went on the grounds of compassion, but I also intended to seek answers to a question that had nagged me for the greater part of my three decades of existence. I wanted to look into the eyes of Mr. Nelson and ask, "Are you my father?" I had discussed it with the cast member with whom I was fasting. I was unsure what the answer would be, but I had a backup plan. I was to hug him and pluck a strand of his hair for a DNA test. That was the surest way to confirm or deny whatever answer he would give me.

When I got to Lartebiokoshie that day, however, the strength to do either of the two things I had elaborately planned and rehearsed in my head deserted me. The sight of Mr. Nelson moved me. Not much had changed about the house since my last visit. The twin one-storey buildings on the compound, which Mr. Nelson and his twin sister had inherited from their parents, still possessed their imposing grandeur and competed with more modern houses in the neighbourhood. The last time I stepped foot in the house was when I was a child in primary school. That was when I vowed never to visit because he had left me in the hall and called his other children to join him in the bedroom. On this day, however, I was in that bedroom with him, alone. If the environment remained the same, a lot had changed about Mr. Nelson, whom I had been told was battling with pneumonia.

He looked all grey and frail. The man I met was a pale impersonation of the buoyant and fun-loving Okoe Nelson, a man who had seen better days in his prime. Apart from his deteriorating health, his wealth seemed to have disappeared, or so it appeared to me. It also seemed there was no woman in his life, which again was a striking irony of his life, for at his peak, he was the ladies' man. It was difficult to reconcile the man I had met on my last visit with the man I was seeing that day.

After I vowed never to visit him, we had met a few times, mostly in the house or at events of his son, Patrick. Patrick Nelson and I got along very well. Of all the children of Mr. Nelson, I had a good relationship with Patrick, Eugene and Sweetie.

I even visited Patrick when I was in London. Not all the children of Okoe Nelson liked me, and it was understandable. His eldest son, for instance, nearly hit me at his funeral. I hadn't met him until that day. He was seething with rage about how I had portrayed his father, our father. He was angry about my public utterances—mostly my media interviews in Ghana and abroad—about the man who was supposed to be my father.

"My father didn't like the interviews you were granting," I remember him telling me, his eyes glinting with anger.

He was right. His father had a good reason not to like what I had said about him. I didn't say kind things about him, but anybody in my shoes wouldn't have acted differently. The interviewers often asked about the influence of my parents in my life and career. Whenever I told them about my mother, they would ask about my father. I couldn't lie about it. I told them he was not in my life. I told them how he had abandoned me and not cared how I turned out. As mild as I tried to be, it turned out to be negative because there was no positive memory to share about my father. I felt that even if he had anything against my mother, he shouldn't have extended that to me, his daughter. I felt he had maltreated me, and I didn't have to go about lying now that I had become a household name. So, the anger of his eldest son was understandable, but he should have understood where I was coming from. If one added my own experience with Mr. Nelson to the stories my mother told me, I couldn't bring myself to love or have any emotional attachment to him.

213

When I sat with him in the room in 2016, however, I couldn't bring myself to hate him either. He sat on the bed and I was sitting across from him. Nothing stood out in our conversation. I could see a man who wanted to make peace with all the people he thought he didn't have a great relationship with. He was calmer and nicer, trying to have a great conversation with me. The absence of a relationship made it a bit awkward and it was a random chat about work and life in general. There was no sign that there was something he wanted to tell me. I could tell he wanted to make peace with me, an attempt he had made in the past but failed.

After I started acting, I sensed a little regret in him. Even if I wasn't his child, I felt he could have acted or behaved differently. He could have treated me more humanely, especially when I was too young to be dragged into whatever unforgivable grudge he held against my mother. This was perhaps the reason he had made an effort to make amends. The most outstanding one was on one of my birthdays when he told my mother that he wanted to have dinner with me. It was his initiative and they booked a table at the Chinese restaurant at the Polo Court near the Accra Mall. He went with my mother to wait for me because I had travelled to Ada with some of my friends earlier in the day. When I returned, I only went to say hi to them and left. I didn't see why I should celebrate my special day with him. I couldn't stand him. Looking back, I think the fact that the two of them came together meant they took that meeting seriously.

214

Seeing him in that state in 2016, however, melted the barrier that stood between us. I knew that even if he survived the ailment, he wouldn't have many more years on earth. That thought was what divided my attention as I chatted with him. I paid attention to his hair, skin, nails, ears and all the features that could give hints about my relationship with him. As I had compared and contrasted since childhood, nothing showed that we were connected in any way. I wished he would tell me something, anything about our relationship. When I failed to hear anything helpful, I left Lartebiokoshie that day and headed for Dansoman.

I had lost count of the number of times I had asked my mother to tell me if Mr. Nelson was, indeed, my father. On this day, however, I went with a renewed determination, buoyed by the encounter with a man in the concluding pages of his life, to put the same question to her. I had received the same answer since I was a child, but I wanted to hear something different.

The truth!

CHAPTER NINETEEN

"Your Father is Peter Ala Adjetey"

I hadn't planned to visit my mother that day. My mission was to go and see Mr. Nelson and execute my agenda before it became too late. However, I couldn't bring myself to ask the ailing man if he was my father. I couldn't muster the courage to pluck a strand of his hair for the DNA test I had intended. The answers I couldn't find from the old man wedged a strong desire in me to find them from the most credible and reliable source. Without the intervention of science, nobody knows the father of a child more than the woman who carried it for nine months.

Lartebiokoshie, where Mr. Nelson lived, isn't far from my mother's house in Dansoman. So, I drove straight there. My mother was in her bedroom when I got to the house that day. She sat on a chair, near the mirror, where her drawer was. I sat on the bed opposite her. I don't remember much of what else we talked about that day, for that was inconsequential. The gravity of what I would leave the house with was enough to subdue the memory of any other subject. The only other thing I remember telling her about was Mr. Nelson's illness. I don't remember whether she said she had already been told about it or she was visiting the old man. Out of the blue, I shot the question as direct as I could.

"Mum, are you sure Mr. Nelson is my father?" I asked in Fante.

"Yvonne, hmmm!" she began.

My heartbeat paused. When it resumed, it missed its rhythm. And quadrupled its speed.

I had hoped and prayed that a day would come when my mother would not dismiss the question and casually recite the same answer like a nursery school rhyme she'd mastered so well and could recall and render even in her sleep. For the first time, however, she gave an indication that she was about to say something different. Yet, I suddenly realised that the truth was as great a burden as the doubt that had plagued my life. I yearned for the truth, but it seemed I wasn't prepared for it. News of that nature is often dropped in clues, in bits and pieces until the heart and mind were prepared enough to take it all in. In some instances, such as bereavement, the recipient of the news is often called in the company of others. Such heavy breaking news is often preceded by comforting words. On this day, however, there was no time for formalities. And my mother proceeded to drop the news as if it was some casual piece of information she was delivering to me.

The man whose surname I carried was not my father, she told me. To me, it wasn't news. It was a confirmation of what I had suspected since I was old enough to reason. The shock of the confirmation still hit me like a thunderbolt. It jostled me out of mental consciousness as I strained to retain my train of thought and proceed to hear the real news. I didn't have enough time to process what that meant for my relationship with Mr. Nelson, the frail man whose house I had just left. The next question was automatic: If it wasn't Mr. Nelson, who, then, was my father?

My mother, who had been tightlipped for over thirty years, was now speaking. It was as if the fasting and prayer had broken her spell of silence, softened her heart and loosened her lips. Whatever had kept her from talking had deserted her, and she was speaking to me.

"Your father is Peter Ala Adjetey," she told me.

"Peter Ala Adjetey?" I said, without knowing how to feel about that.

"Yes," she said.

Under normal circumstances, I would have asked who that man was. She was telling me about him for the first time. But if the Peter Ala Adjetey I knew was the one she was referring to—and that was the

218

man she meant—he needed no introduction. Peter Ala Adjetey was a household name, a name that retained its brand and identity only when it was mentioned in full. He wasn't Peter or Ala. And there are thousands of Adjeteys so he wasn't Mr. Adjetey. He was Peter Ala Adjetey. At the time my mother announced him as my father, he had died eight years earlier. Any Ghanaian of my generation who didn't know or hadn't heard about Peter Ala Adjetey had, perhaps, lived a greater part of their lives in space. If there was nothing to recall about him at all, the unmistakable howl of his baritone voice calling parliament to order was a common feature in comedy.

Born in 1931, Peter Ala Adjetey became one of the most prominent lawyers in Ghana. In the Third Republic of Ghana, in the early 1980s, he was a member of parliament. In the Fourth Republic when the NPP won the historic December 2000 election from the NDC, he was made the Speaker of Parliament. He served from January 2001 to January 2005 and passed away three years later.

It wasn't Peter Ala Adjetey the politician my mother had met. It was Peter Ala Adjetey the lawyer. He was her attorney during her divorce from her first husband, the father of my two siblings. That's how the two met and got intimate along the line, my mother told me. She proceeded to tell me where and how it all happened, as a result of which I was conceived. It happened once, she emphasised, as if that mattered to me. She did not, however, tell me the circumstances under which I didn't become Yvonne Adjetey. She fast-forwarded the story to ten years after my birth when she said she had discovered I was the daughter of Peter Ala Adjetey. When I asked why she had kept that away from me, she had an explanation.

She initially wanted to tell me, she explained. I was ten years old at the time and she felt the need to let me in on who my father was. But the man she consulted advised against it. That man, one Pastor Wiafe, had often prayed with her. When she sought a second opinion from him, he said it was not necessary. I was only ten. Peter Ala Adjetey was married. And she didn't have to disrupt the present by stirring up an unpleasant past, Pastor Wiafe advised. The decision, therefore, was to keep me in the dark forever.

Even before those words worked up my soul, mind and heart like the venom of a scorpion, my mother's attitude was what hurt me most. To tell a 31-year-old woman that the man you've always presented to her isn't her true father needs to be taken seriously. To tell her that the man you've caused her to hate and fight all these years isn't her father must come with an apology. This is the kind of news you break by first apologising, holding and consoling your daughter and asking for forgiveness even if you had a good reason to keep the news away from her. My mother didn't do any of these. She broke the news as casually as though she was telling me about a routine visit to the dentist. There was no apology. There was no trace of remorse in her voice or on her face. Nothing. She just said it, dropped the topic and jumped on to something else.

I left Dansoman after about five minutes of hearing the news. My mind was too agitated to process what I had heard. My heart was too heavy to contain it. And my mouth would have been too quick to respond to the pain if I had stayed longer and interrogated her further. I might have ended up saying something irreversibly hurtful to her. I avoided that by leaving.

The drive from Dansoman to my house was the longest 36-kilometre journey I had made in my life. I still do not know how I got home in one piece, without a dent on my vehicle or body. It was one of those occasions you become a passenger of the vehicle you are driving, an occasion when your limbs are detached from your senses but somehow manage to steer you home safely because they are familiar with the route. My mind became a playground for all manner of thoughts—positive, negative, unforgiveness and conciliatory—that came running in and out at will. I struggled to process what I had heard.

I was somehow relieved that my relentlessness had yielded positive results. I could now understand why Mr. Nelson treated me with so much disdain. I was also beginning to resent my mother. Why did she have to listen to a pastor? I felt she was old enough to have decided what was good for her and her daughter without succumbing to the ill advice from the pastor.

Why did she think I didn't have to know the truth? Even if she didn't think having a father figure in my life meant anything, the fact that her other two children had a father in their lives should have reminded her that I could be hurt by seeing them and hearing them talk about their father. Did she really care about me? Was she really my mother? I hadn't doubted that, but I was beginning to wonder why I had been treated differently. I wondered why she had given me the impression that I somehow merited the treatment she subjected me to when I had no hand in anything that happened before I was born. I started to think about how she had told me many times that she had given birth to me by mistake and even said the medical doctor who saved my life by opting out of the initial plan to abort me was still alive.

If what I had heard that day gave me hope that I would finally bring closure to my identity and pick up the fragments of my life and move on, one thought assailed me and undid whatever positive feeling that came with the news of that day. As faint as it was, it dominated every other thought that came with the news. It was the possibility that what my mother told me could be untrue. If she could lie to me in the past, then she could lie to me now. But to what end? What would she gain? What would she achieve? Was it because Peter Ala Adjetey was dead and Mr. Nelson didn't look like someone who had enough time on his hands to dabble in our drama? But why would she lie about Peter Ala Adjetey when she could have left it unsaid? Was there a way to find the truth when the man was long gone?

When I got home that day, I locked myself up in the room for three days, only interrupting the solitary confinement by visiting the refrigerator to pick something I could munch on. I wanted to be alone, with my phone and the internet as my only companions. My mother did not call that day to find out how I was or what I was going through after she broke the news to me. She did not call the following day or the third. She never called to empathise or sympathise with me over the unwholesome discovery of which she was both the source and cause. I thought she should have understood the weight of what she had told me. I couldn't talk to anybody at that point. Considering who I was, anything of this nature that leaked was going to be news, and that would compound my woes. Ours is an industry with an enormous trust deficit. Talking to random friends about this issue was as good as talking to entertainment reporters and bloggers. So, before I figured out whom I could confide in, the only person I needed to talk to was my mother. I needed to hear from her. I needed love and consolation at that moment. If I had been starved of fatherly love, then the love of my mother should comfort me in the most difficult time of my life. That remained a vain wish.

I had to bear my burden alone, but I wasn't idle. I set to work immediately after I got home. I turned myself into a forensic scientist, analysing every detail and body feature of Peter Ala Adjetey in the photos I found on the internet. I googled him and read everything there was to read about him. I pored over the tons of images that Google threw at me when I typed the name and hit the image search. The internet was invented in his old age so it was almost impossible to find images of his youthful years, photos in which I could spot a modicum of resemblance. What worsened the situation was that most of the photos were either pixilated or were photos of him as the speaker of parliament in which almost all his body was covered in the colonial robes bequeathed to our political system by the British, whose political system we copied and badly modified to cater to the benefit of the tiny minority of rulers.

One of the photos, however, stood out. It was a photograph of Peter Ala Adjetey with one of his children, Petrina Adjetey, who had graduated from a university in London. As I looked at the photos of a proud father and his happy daughter, I didn't only focus on the physical features I needed to confirm my mother's story. I also imagined myself in Petrina's place. The man looked caring and responsible. If he could travel all the way to London to be part of his daughter's graduation, what could he not do for me? For a moment, I imagined myself in that photograph. My short stay in the fantasy world was interrupted by the urgency of my mission. I still had a lot of work to do. I needed to confirm the news first before brooding over what I had missed.

Even without Googling, I knew Peter Ala Adjetey was tall, but that's where our similarities ended. It was when I spoke to former President John Agyekum Kufuor that he pointed out other invisible features that linked me to the politician he had worked closely with. Before that, however, I sent Petrina a message on Facebook, through the account that shared the photos I focused on.

"Hello Sweets," I began. "Hope you are doing well, [I] want to have a word with you. Kindly reply with your number. Yvonne Nelson."

Shortly after that, I sent her another message with my mobile phone number so that she could WhatsApp me because I received many messages through social media and might miss her reply on Facebook. I sent my message on December 3, 2016, but no response came. I checked my WhatsApp anytime a strange number texted me, but none of them ever introduced themselves as Petrina Adjetey.

After a while, I sent another message, "Hello Petrina."

Petrina finally responded on August 11, 2021. But it wasn't the response I wanted. She said, "I am not sure of the genuineness of this message."

She would later tell me she thought it was someone else who wanted to scam her by impersonating me. She didn't think the "popular Yvonne Nelson" would send her a message trying to initiate a chat with her. I couldn't fault her. It was even better I didn't add why I needed to connect with her. The reason I needed to talk to her sounded like a scammer's tale. But I had to do it even if they would not believe me.

Reaching out to Peter Ala Adjetey's children was something I dreaded and had to tread with trepidation. The man was no more, so it was easy for someone to show up with a one-sided story about him. That could upset his children and family. The only consolation was that this was happening eight good years after the man's death when his will would have been long executed. Besides, I was Yvonne Nelson, not a miserable soul who wanted to feed on whatever the man had left behind.

When I came out of my self-imposed incarceration, I decided to speak to people. I spoke to my brother about it, but, like my mother, he showed no emotions. I expected him to feel sorry for me, comfort or console me, but that didn't happen. It was my sister who did what I had expected from my brother and mother. She was concerned and empathetic. She tried to cheer me up and help me to forget whatever had happened and move on with my life.

My nanny was distraught when I told her the story. She was hit hard by the story as if it was her own predicament. She shared her own story of growing up and having to endure life with others while her parents were alive. She wept as my story unfolded. I later told my friends, Nana Akua and Fianko Bossman. Before all the others came in, however, I decided to speak to one man I thought knew the late Peter Ala Adjetey well and could provide some clues.

President John Agyekum Kufuor had had a hand in the nomination of Peter Ala Adjetey as the second Speaker of Parliament of the Fourth Republic of Ghana. He was subsequently voted by members of parliament and sworn into office. Prior to that, Peter Ala Adjetey had served as the national chairman of the NPP from 1995 to 1998 and worked with Mr. Kufuor in that capacity, so the two knew each other well. Before the Fourth Republic, both men had been politicians in the 1980s, so I was speaking to the right man.

Former President Kufuor did not have any reason to doubt my mother's story. He said he had monitored my Dumsor-Must-Stop

226

campaign, and if anyone said I was related to Peter Ala Adjetey, he could tell where I got my strength of conviction from. He encouraged me not to let my past hold me down. He was happy I had not turned out to be a failure as a result of the absence of the late statesman in my life. He said I should focus on building on whatever gains I had made and not brood over things I had no control over. He opened his doors to me and assured me of a listening ear if I ever needed any. I left feeling somewhat happy or relieved, but it was temporary.

There are certain things that don't leave you no matter how hard you try. I spent the days after the news going back and forth on what I had heard. Why was my mother opening up now? I had no answer. I thought about how I had lived my entire life with a fake identity. I was not Yvonne Nelson, but I could not be sure that I was Yvonne Adjetey either. Like the fruit bat, I wasn't sure whether I was a mammal or a bird. I was just hanging in there, hoping things would normalise so I could know where I belonged, but I knew that I wasn't the type to allow things to slide. I had come too far to trust easily. So, as the pain and shock subsided, I plotted my next move.

CHAPTER TWENTY

DNA Tests with Peter Ala Adjetey's children

After my initial attempt at reaching the children of Peter Ala Adjetey failed, it took nearly five years before I started to seriously pursue them again. The encouragement and advice of former President Kufuor had calmed and lulled me into thinking I could forget about the shocking revelation from my mother and move on with my life. However, the urge to know who my father truly was became an unavoidable perennial visitor to my mind. Whenever it came around, it took hold of my being and made me restless. It filled me with doubts and questions that needed to be put to rest. What often stood out on those occasions was the question about whether my mother could lie to me again. What motivation would she have to tell me about a second man being my father if it wasn't true? The answer to that question was even louder. If she could lie to me the first time, she could lie to me the second time. At that stage of my life, I was old enough to know the truth and not swallow my mother's words hook, line and sinker. The thought of finding an alternative truth often scared and sank me, but I made a move.

I first reached out to Kiki Banson for the number of Gabby Adjetey. I knew he would have Gabby's contact because Kiki was (and still is) a big name and well-connected figure in Ghana's entertainment industry. Gabby Adjetey, who is now in London, once worked with Joy FM so I was certain Kiki would have his number. Kiki expressed his shock when I told him the story and why I needed Gabby's number. I, however, told him it was classified information, and he promised to keep it as such.

Two days after getting his number, I set up a video call with Gabby. At that point, I had become conscious of the never-ending drama, so I decided to document my search. I set up a camera and recorded myself making the call in what was to be my first encounter with my real father's child. I didn't have to struggle to introduce myself because Gabby knew who I was. What he did not know and would not have imagined was what I was about to tell him, that I was his sister.

I began by issuing a disclaimer. I told him I was not making that call because I needed anything from him or his family. I told him that, by the grace of God, I was self-sufficient and content with what I had. I was not interested in the inheritance of a man I had never met. Gabby was kind and receptive. He smiled throughout our conversation, and I remember him asking whether his father knew about me. He said before his father passed, he brought in a child he had fathered "outside" and introduced to the family. He wondered why he never mentioned me. He said that did not in any way suggest he doubted my story, but he was unsure his father—or rather our father— knew about my relationship with him while he was alive. I told him I was not sure my mother had mentioned it to him. What mattered most was that I had reached out, he said. If the response from Gabby was anything to go by, then I had been accepted by the Ala Adjeteys. He even joked about the fact that he had been "spying" on me for a long time and if he had made a move, it would have been a disaster now that we knew we were related.

Gabby and I ended our conversation with a discussion on the next move. Larry Adjetey, also a lawyer, was the head of the family, he told me. It was imperative that I told him everything I had discussed with him (Gabby). He gave me Larry's number and promised to put a word through to him.

Larry was receptive, kind and welcoming. The initial uneasiness and nervousness I had harboured about a possible rejection disappeared when I spoke with him. It had eased considerably after my conversation with Gabby. Larry invited me over for a special welcome lunch and got a chef to make a special pizza for me. I went with my daughter, nanny, and my manager, Francis. Petrina and Franklin Adjetey were there too. The Adjeteys and their families went the extra mile to ensure that I felt at home, literally. But as we dined and wined, my mind constantly strayed away from the dining table and took on an investigative task that had started long before I heard about my

230

relationship with the Adjeteys. I had constantly looked out for clues that proved my relationship with Mr. Nelson. My mother's revelation that he was not my father had proven me right. It gave me a firmer reason to trust my instinct, observation and commonsense analysis. Those tools were at work while I shared a table of love and kindness with the Adjeteys. They accepted me as part of them, but I didn't take anything for granted. That acceptance did not prove any biological relationship between us.

The feelers of my six senses were, therefore, wide awake to hints of resemblance, mannerisms or anything that suggested otherwise. As I probed, I realised there was very little to show that I was from this family. Their noses, foreheads, cheeks and eyes did not look like mine. Frankie and Gabby, for instance, bore a resemblance that strongly suggested a blood relationship, but there was no one among them that looked like me. The kinky hair was not enough, in my view. In my part of the world, it is the normal human hair, and sharing that trait with someone means nothing.

After lunch, I took a tour of the living room, pretending to admire the paintings and family portraits and other photos, but I was looking for something more than that. I didn't want to make it so obvious that I was scanning those images for something deeper than what they meant. It was when I moved from one image to the other that I saw a photo of young Peter Ala Adjetey. It was a black-and-white photograph of him when he graduated from law school. I had hoped that that one could give me the clues I need but it drew a blank.

By the end of that lunch, I had enough doubts to get me worried. And I thought they might also have their own doubts too. They are a bunch of intelligent men and women. They knew their father and must have known that I was not anywhere close to the features of their father or any of his children. If they didn't have doubts about my story, then it meant they had given me the benefit of the doubt. I was tall and their father was tall, and they may have believed I looked like my mother. But I was convinced there was more to my mother's claim that Peter Ala Adjetey was my father.

The Adjeteys showered me with love. The entire family was very sweet. I felt lucky to be part of them and Larry's parting words were reassuring.

"This is your family," he told me. "You've met us. Don't hesitate to come home any time you want to," he told me.

Growing up, I don't remember my brother ever hugging or embracing me with affection. Getting this from the Adjeteys meant a lot to me. The other part of me was, however, asking questions, analysing the love shown me and subjecting it to scrutiny. I had got to a phase of my life when people could act around me. The industry I found myself in also did not make me appreciate it when people were showing genuine love. I didn't really trust anyone, the reason I kept asking questions even though the family welcomed me with open arms. Could it be because I was a celebrity? Would they have done the same if I had been an ordinary lady who walked into the family with this story?

232

My desire for definitive answers grew when I left the residence of Larry Adjetey. I called up Fianko Bossman and told him I was considering a DNA test. With doubts hanging like gloomy clouds, I was uneasy about being considered a family member of the Adjeteys. I told him I needed to be sure I wasn't an imposter. The thought of the DNA test with the children of Peter Ala Adjetey was like a eureka moment for me. I was surprised that it hadn't crossed my mind to do the test with Eugene Nelson when I had my doubts and was old enough to find out. Fianko was not enthused about the idea though.

"Yvonne, your mum has told you the truth. What else are you looking for?" he asked me on the phone. He was in the United States at the time.

"If my mum could lie to me the first time, then she could lie to me the second time," I responded in a way that was more of a reassurance to myself that I was about to do the right thing than a reply to his question.

One day, I called Petrina and Franklin and told them about my intention to have a DNA test with them. Petrina and I had developed a great relationship. She was a very nice lady. We had great conversations. She told me about growing up, how my supposed father had been and how he had treated them. Sometimes, she got emotional recounting her fond memories of the man who was considered a statesman, the man they shared with Ghana and should have shared with me.

I got to know Peter Ala Adjetey through the stories his children told me. He loved education and wanted all his children to be well-educated. He was biased towards law. If I had been introduced to him earlier, and if he had accepted me as his child, he would probably have encouraged me to read law. I don't know how I would have fared in that profession and what that would have meant for my love for the entertainment industry. At the time these "if" clauses filled almost every sentence that formed in my mind, however, my preoccupation was how to put every doubt to rest, even if some people thought it was not necessary.

Petrina was one of them. To her, I was subjecting myself to needless stress. What mattered was that I had met the family and they had unreservedly accepted me. I, on the other hand, told her it was the necessary thing to do. It felt unusually odd to just wake up and go to tell them I was their father's child and be accepted without any proof. They were not worried, but I was. I wanted to end the doubt that was building up in my world like a wild anthill.

Petrina and Franklin were kind enough to agree to my request to do the test. I could have done it with one of them, but out of an abundance of caution, I decided to have the test with both of them. The next step was how to do it "safely". I didn't want to walk to a health facility with the two for the DNA test. It could create attention and someone could leak it. I was not yet prepared to face the world in that regard. I was still fighting my own internal battles and could not afford to have a media frenzy out of the situation. For that singular reason, I opted for home service and, on the said date, my two new siblings were in my house for the test.

I do not know how they felt about it, but, to me, it was an issue of great importance. I felt uneasy and grim about the exercise. It was like the pregnancy test I had taken many years ago when I wasn't ready for a baby. I dreaded a particular outcome, but I was better off knowing about it. November 17, which had meant nothing to me would suddenly become a crucial date in my life, the date I initiated something concrete about my identity. If it turned out well, that date in 2021 would be engraved in my heart and mind as the date I took a definitive step and found closure. That was my wish when the man from the DNA company followed the Google map I had sent him to my house.

He started with Petrina. He took her name and bio-data and recorded everything. He then produced a swab and asked her to open her mouth. Covid-19 had made such procedures common, but it was still uncomfortable. He rubbed the swab deep into her mouth, in the right and left corners of her cheeks and then placed the sample in a container and labeled it. He repeated the same procedure on Franklin and then came to me last.

The process did not last long, but the time we spent awaiting the result seemed to have outlasted eternity. He said it would take up to ten days, but the ten days were like ten months. The notification finally came on November 29, 2021. It set my heart throbbing like a drum. It was sent via WhatsApp and email. I was then given a password to open each of the two pdf files, and I did so with trembling hands. The fear was palpable.

The first one I opened was captioned "DNA Profiling Test Report." The test was described as "half sibling test".

I didn't have time to read the long narration and explanation that came with the result. I needed the conclusion or something to the effect that it was either positive or negative. That was provided in three different ways, in addition to the long narrative. The portion market "Result" said: "Not supportive of half siblings."

The conclusion said, "The likelihood obtained is not supportive of the relationship tested."

There was a third summary titled "statement", which read: "The DNA profiles... comprising alleles observed at the tested DNA markers, were compared to calculate the likelihood that they share a half sibling relationship. The calculated likelihood of <0.001 does not support the hypothesis that the tested individuals share a half sibling relationship."

I didn't need any expert to tell me what this meant. My heart had got the message and was threatening to pound my chest open and come out to face the world, and perhaps my mother, for subjecting it to such torture. But my mind had a consolation that tried in vain to calm my heart. I had done two tests. The fact that one did not support the hypothesis did not mean the other would not. So, I set to work on opening the other test result, the one with Franklin.

It was not different from that of my DNA test with Petrina.

CHAPTER TWENTY-ONE

Another DNA Test

It took me more than a week to soak in the shock that nearly ruined my sanity. I could not sleep, but whenever I managed to catch a nap, I would wake up trembling with panic attacks. Those attacks came from a number of unresolved questions and the mess I had made by introducing myself to the children of Peter Ala Adjetey. They and their families and, perhaps, some friends had been told that I was one of them. How was I going to look them in the eye and say I was not their sibling as I had claimed? The fear of facing them did not, however, break me like the reality that my mother had lied to me the second time.

The more I struggled with the pain, the more I felt as though my dad was somewhere close, urging me to find him. I felt strongly he was not dead. I felt as though a part of me was somewhere, as if a voice was calling out to me saying, "I'm not so far away. Search harder, and you will find me."

I began to imagine what kind of man my father could be. Maybe he was somebody I had met. He was probably someone I met in my childhood or someone I knew but did not know we were related.

I was determined to keep searching and to keep fighting. The truth would not be hidden forever. It was like an itch I could not reach with my own hands to scratch. I was not going to give up even if the hand that could help me—my mother—was unwilling. Or was she mocking me? Was she enjoying my misery? Did she not know how intensely I felt about the same question I had been asking since I was a child? The answers to these questions I asked myself proved as elusive as the identity of my father. In the midst of the confusion and heartache, I had to pause and deal with the family I had invited into my own mess. I had to tell the Adjeteys the truth.

Petrina had been asking about the results since the day we tested. She appeared as anxious as I was, perhaps, not with the same amount of gravity I treated the test. She was proving to be that loving and caring sister I never had. She was hurt when I told her the outcome of the DNA test.

After telling Franklin and Petrina, I sent Larry a text message to announce the news. As far as the result of the DNA test was concerned, I sent all of them WhatsApp messages, for I couldn't bear to speak to them. To say I was embarrassed is an understatement. The Adjeteys were worried and felt sorry for me. I knew their nuclear families would be disappointed too. For days, and perhaps weeks, I would be the subject matter of discussion at the dining table, in the living rooms and in the beds of the family that had embraced me. And was the story going to end there or would it find its way out of an unguarded tongue and spill into the gossip mill of an industry that survives on such juicy gossips? How was I going to relate with them going forward? Could I act as though I had never met them or was I to pretend we were still family and continue to bask in their generosity and love?

For instance, Larry's wife used to cook for me. On one occasion when I was supposed to go there for lunch and I couldn't make it, his driver brought the food to me. I could sense it was specially made for me. His daughter came to visit. Either Larry's daughter or wife made candles. He gave me some, for I love candles. It would be cruel to cut these lovely people off because of the test, but the closer I got, the more I was reminded of my shame and pain.

After I sent them the messages, they all flooded my phone with calls, but I was not in the mood to speak, and they respected my request for privacy. When it got better, I spoke with them and they assured me that they still considered me one of them despite the absence of a biological relationship. Their doors were open to me, they said, and I didn't need to be convinced that these were people who loved me genuinely. I appreciated their love, but to help me cope with my own battles, I needed to withdraw as quietly as I had sneaked into their lives. I asked for space without saying it, and they respected it.

I made them know it was hard for me. Larry did not stop reaching out to me. He emphasised that we were still family. He is still warm and welcoming, and so are his other siblings with whom I had come into contact. That did not stop me from probing further for my real family.

My search continued after the disappointing outcome with the Adjeteys. It occurred to me that, up to that point, I had not scientifically tested my relationship with Nelsons. I had not gathered the courage to take Mr. Nelson's sample for a DNA test before he passed, but I knew his children. I was also now armed with enough information about DNA to know that I could put the matter to rest on that score. I decided to give it a try, for what if Mr. Nelson was actually my father and I kept running around searching for someone else?

As expected, there was only one person I was close to and comfortable enough to make that request of. I called Eugene and told him my intention. I told him I needed his help, but he needed to keep the outcome a secret because I wasn't ready to put it out there. Eugene understood me and did not object to the DNA test. The DNA scientist took Eugene and me through the same routine he had taken the Adjeteys and me. The major difference now was that the two of us who were testing for this "alleged" relationship shared the same surname.

The result came on December 16, 2021. And it was the same as the one with the Adjeteys. No relationship was established.

Neither Eugene nor I was surprised at the outcome of the test. My mother had told me Mr. Nelson was not my father and, from my own analysis, I had no reason to doubt her. The test was to eliminate any possibility that I was related to them. And with that result, I got closure on that side, even if that closure was in only one leg of the puzzle. There was nothing linking me to the Nelsons and the fact that my mother had told me about it five years earlier made it easier to cope with the pain much better than I did with the Adjeteys' results.

Even before the DNA test, I had got some closure with the Nelsons. When, in 2021, the family said they were sharing Mr. Nelson's estate, I told them I was not interested in any property he had left behind. Eugene had told me that the lawyer wanted all his children to know that his properties were about to be shared, but I told him I didn't need anything. He said the lawyer insisted I put my response in writing and I did. My mother had already told me Mr. Nelson wasn't my father. Even if she hadn't told me, I still wouldn't have wanted anything from him. I thought he had denied me what I needed most—fatherly love— and I didn't want to have anything to do with the property of a man who didn't want to have anything to do with me as his child.

When, in early 2017, Mr. Nelson died, his family said the children should make monetary contributions to perform the funeral. I resented the whole idea, but I still gave my contribution. I had just got confirmation from my mother that he was not my father, but what they were asking for wasn't too much to give. I didn't want to abstain and create another scene and talking point.

The attempt by his first son to hit me at the "one-week" ceremony of his passing, however, kept me thinking about whether any of his children did not know the truth. The mother of that son had chased Eugene and me out of the house when we went to visit Patrick. She wielded either a knife or a stick (I can't recall clearly). She was Mr. Nelson's first wife and appeared well-to-do. Our presence, however, seemed to remind her of some pain and resentment against Mr. Nelson, which she could not overcome. Patrick, because of whom Eugene and I were in the house, was one of her sons. We had left the house shocked and terrified. It only compounded the complications in my relationship with the Nelsons. Here was a woman thinking that our mothers had ruined her marriage or something to that effect. I could not say much for Eugene's mother, but I knew my mother didn't have anything positive to say about Mr. Nelson.

The result of the DNA test, therefore, brought an end to all this drama. I now knew if I had to lay claim to a father, then I had to continue to search. The time to nurse the faintest possibility of Mr. Nelson being my father was long gone. I had to get further clues, some lifeline with which to proceed with another investigation that would probably end with a DNA test. At this point, I hoped I could get another source to point me in a different and more truthful direction. I needed someone who knew the truth and was prepared to share it with me. But is there anyone who knows the paternity of a child more than the mother of that child? My mother had told me two names. Neither of them turned out to be my father.

Did she not know the truth herself? Was she unsure who my father was? Did she know but decided that I should not know? Was my father a man she was not proud to have had a relationship with? And if that was the case, would she be willing to divulge something she had fought against all the time I had asked her? Should I just ignore her and do my own search? But where and how would I begin?

I finally decided that if there would be any further step, I had to go back to the source that had the answers. It was time to confront my mother with my findings.

CHAPTER TWENTY-TWO

Confronting My Mother

I got to my mother's house by 6 a.m. It was a time I was certain she would be at home. I was right. She had just woken up and probably sensed the urgency of my visit. It was early and unannounced. It had taken me some time after the DNA tests to conclude that I needed to confront her. I took even more time to rehearse my encounter with her. I went with my manager, but he was outside. I was alone with my mother in the room. She had extended the house so her bedroom was now housed in the new compartment she had added to the house. I sat on the bed while she sat on the chair.

I went prepared. I was armed with three DNA test results. I was also armed with Bible verses. They were quotations about love, forgiveness and how the Bible wants Christians to coexist. She was happy to see me and was even happier when I began our meeting with the Bible. I had grown up knowing her fondness for the word of God, especially after her motor accident in my secondary school days. She is a prominent member of the Methodist Church, and the Bible is her refuge in times of trouble. She is one of those who are not ashamed of the gospel and want everyone around them to know it. The sacred book and its power mean an awful lot to her and seeing her daughter start a visit with quotations from the Bible might have suggested to her that I had got to the stage of my spirituality that she had probably prayed about.

She lightened up and made an attempt to pick up her own Bible, but I told her it was not necessary, for I was the one going to do all the reading. I began with the verses of the sacred book that talked about forgiveness. Then I proceeded to love and godly coexistence. I was composed in a way that surprised me.

I had every reason to be furious. She had deceived me twice and I had found the truth. But I had learned enough to know that getting angry would not get me anywhere in my search. I needed her. She was the holder of the truth, and even if she was not sure, she could give me pointers to establish the truth on my own. If I ruined that avenue, my search would be impaired forever. If I put all that aside, she was still my mother, and the last thing I would want to do was to disrespect her. So, I kept calm and read one scripture after the other until I had exhausted the list of quotations I had written, about ten of them.

As I proceeded, her mood switched from gladness to apprehension. She sensed it wasn't a morning devotion or some positive news that I had decided to start with quotations from the religious book. When I was done, I told her, as calmly as I could, the reason for my visit. I showed her the DNA test results and told her their contents, extending them to her for verification if she doubted me. I then proceeded to tell her in an imploring tone that I needed her to tell me who my father was.

She burst into a tirade of accusation and abuse. She told me she knew I was up to something. She said she had dreamt that I would disgrace her, and what was unfolding that morning was not new to her. I was not going to fall for any form of emotional blackmail and I made her know it. I told her she probably knew I would search and find answers beyond her words. To dream about it meant her God was talking to her, I told her. It was the reason she should tell me the truth so that we both bring closure to the subject.

She was not ready to listen to me. The tirade continued, even after I reminded her that I had not come there to fight, the reason I came with Bible verses. I wanted us to talk like a mother and daughter, like two mature human beings who respected each other and saw the need to find a solution that was available. The solution was in her bosom.

No amount of appeal to my mother worked. She started to act strangely. I could not tell whether it was genuine or fake, but she looked like someone who had suddenly become sick and weak. She asked me to get off the bed so she could lie down, but I resisted. I told her she should let us exhaust the subject, but she would not listen. She turned away from me, and, after some time, stood up. I tried to hug her but she resisted me. When I held her, she turned away. All this while, she kept telling me to leave if I had finished saying what I had come to say to her.

After some time, she stopped talking and asked me to say all that I had to say and leave. I had no option, so I obliged. I went back to my car and left without the answers I needed. Sacking me from her house ruined our relationship and caused me to lose much of the love I had for her. I have not gone to her house since then, and she, too, has not stepped foot in my house since that encounter. Ryn, however, still goes to her though. I do not allow whatever friction we have to deny my daughter the opportunity to see her grandmother. Any time she feels like seeing her, I send her with my nanny. Sometimes, she spends days before returning.

It has been more than a year since I saw my mother. Our last communication was on my birthday in 2022. She sent me a WhatsApp message wishing me a happy birthday: "Happy birthday my love. May the God of heaven continue to bless you in all your endeavours in Jesus' name. Enjoy your day to the fullest."

My response was: "If you truly love me, you will tell me who my father is. I'm 37 years. You have been unfair to me. This is the LAST time I will ever ask you."

And I have since not asked her. I have given up hope that she will ever open up. Since she told me to leave her house, I have been blinded by what I consider wickedness, her decision to deny me the knowledge of my father. I can't imagine myself doing that to my daughter. I do not know why she could do this to me in my entire life. I do not understand her. Whoever my father is, whatever surrounds my birth, I deserve to know. If it's bad, and if telling me would hurt me, that's my dad. That's my story. I need to be told.

My mother's behaviour has erased almost every positive feeling I had for her from my mind. Anytime I want to attach emotions to her, I get blocked by her refusal to tell me who my father is. When I had my daughter and had sleepless nights and postpartum depression, I developed so much respect and appreciation for my mother. I still do. I used to call and ask her how she managed to do this on three different occasions.

Her first two childbirths might have been easier, I often guessed. Going through it the third time without the presence and support of my father must have been tough. I had experienced a bit of it, so I sympathised with her. My own experience made me understand and forgive her for whatever mistakes she might have made. It's not in my place to judge her. She was young, in her 20s. She was vulnerable and could even have been taken advantage of. I have not walked a metre in her shoes and do not blame her for any mistakes she might have made. I don't know how I would have fared in her place. But, still, that does not give her the right to deny me knowledge of my father.

I do not think she is oblivious to how it feels to be in my shoes. She has been there before. She discovered who her father was before he died.

If it wasn't important, she wouldn't have gone searching even after bearing three children. I expected her to understand me, to appreciate how I felt. She knows how it all began, how a basic school teacher first alerted me to something I did not know and set me on a lifelong search. She should have known that telling me all the terrible things about Mr. Nelson, making us enemies and later revealing to me that he wasn't my father would hurt me. She should have known that intruding into other people's families and lives and having eggs on my face because I wasn't related to them as she had made me believe would hurt any grown-up. She should have known that a child who had searched for her father this long and had been deceived twice was a wounded soul and her duty was to help her heal.

It's either she doesn't know the extent to which I have suffered emotionally and psychologically over this or she just doesn't care. She doesn't care about my mental health, because even after I vowed to cut her off, there was one more attempt to appeal to her heart.

That step was taken by Fianko, who had seen me online at odd hours. He reached out after some time to find out if all was well with me because he saw me online when I ought to be sleeping. (He was in the United States so my odd hours were his usual working hours.) I opened up to him and told him everything that was happening to me. The results of the DNA tests were taking a toll on me. I was struggling to sleep and cope with life. He volunteered to reach out to my mother and let her appreciate how I was feeling, how I was reeling under the weight of pain. He would then beg her to help me bring closure to the issue. I didn't object to his offer to intervene because I needed it, and he did intervene.

He told my mother that I was suffering emotionally. He begged her to open up to me and help me. Any mother would have reached out, but it has been seven months since the last attempt to touch her heart, and she has still not called. It hurts to think that she doesn't care how I feel or what happens to me.

It hurts to know that I don't know my father and don't know of any other family or heritage to which I belong. The only parent I know has set a sharp razor on the bond that held us together all these years. I have no idea how it will end or what the future of our relationship will be like.

But I feel it keeps getting worse, and it may not improve until my mother is ready to tell me who my father is. I am not Yvonne Nelson. I need to know who I am.

CHAPTER TWENTY-THREE

An Apology to Mr. Nelson

Dear Mr. Okoe Nelson,

I do not know where to begin this and what it will achieve, but I feel strongly about it. I know I have to do it. I feel I owe you an apology, even if the timing is wrong and my apology may mean nothing to you. But, wherever you are, find a place in your heart to forgive me.

I became resentful towards you because of what my mother told me about you. I had no reason to doubt her because when I made attempts to get close to you, your rejection only confirmed her claim that you didn't like me. At one point, I even thought you hated me. I knew you and my mother were not on good terms, but I did not deserve to be treated like a piece of rag by my father. That's how I saw your reaction towards me.

One cannot blame a child who constantly heard that her dad did not like her. That child would obviously grow up detesting him. I did not understand why a man would hate his own offspring. It was the reason I painted you black in a number of media interviews I granted. That was all the information I had about you. Though I didn't go to the extreme, I spoke the truth. You were not part of my life and I did not hesitate to say that publicly. At the time, I was right.

However, I have now come to understand that you had no reason to be part of my life at all. You owed me nothing, not even your surname. I have come to know the truth and realised that you may have had your own battles as far as I was concerned. You were not my father and I was not your daughter.

To you, your children and your family, I sincerely apologise. I'm sorry that I said all those things about you. I wish you were alive so I could say this to you in person. I first heard from my mother that you were not my father when I visited you in the concluding part of 2016, during the dying embers of your life. I was still in shock. Before I confirmed the truth, you were gone.

I regret I couldn't apologise to you in person. Although the first apology should have come from my mother, I wish I could kneel by you and tell you how sorry I am. But that is not the only reason I wish you were around. I would have loved to know whether you knew the truth. I would have loved to hear whether you knew I was not your daughter, and more importantly, if you knew of someone else who probably could be my father. I would have asked why you never raised it with me. That would have ended the animosity and the bad blood between us.

Now, all that is not necessary. I now know the truth, even if the back story will forever remain hidden. I wish things had not been this way. I ask for your forgiveness, wherever you are. Forgive me that I dragged your name in the mud.

Yours sincerely,
Yvonne.

CHAPTER TWENTY-FOUR

A Letter to My Father

Dear Dad,

I cannot tell you how many times I have cried because I do not know you. I have tried to be strong. Growing up, I tried to shake off derogatory comments and names such as "abanoma", but the more I tried, the more I was reminded of the reality that I did not know my father.

I have a strong feeling that you exist. I feel you're still alive. I pray to God to give you long life and cause our paths to cross before you pass on to eternity. I have a feeling you know me, so if you see me, don't pass by. Come forward and let me see you.

The main reason I wrote this book is to find you. I could have gone on social media or mainstream media to announce it, but that would have left out the backstories. No social media post or mainstream media interview could have captured my journey and struggle from the day the teacher called Eugene and me to his desk to ask if our father was the same man. That innocent instigation has helped me to establish what was not. I now want to know what is, who my father is.

I have carried a false identity. I now know I am not Yvonne Nelson. What I don't know is the surname that I was to supposed to carry.

Perhaps, if I had known you, it wouldn't have been a big deal. I would never have understood anyone who goes through depression in search of her father even at a time she is self-reliant and is able to take care of others. Having endured it for close to four decades, I understand it better. That's why I'm reaching out to you. It doesn't matter the circumstances surrounding my birth. If you are out there, reach out to me.

When King Ayisoba burst onto the Ghanaian music scene with "I Want to See You, My Father", many found it amusing. But I find myself having to repeat those same words. I want to see you, daddy. I want to hear from you. I want to know more about myself. Scientists say the male chromosomes determine the sex of the child. I don't regret the woman I have become and I will be happy to see the man who contributed in some way to who I am today. I don't care about who you are or the circumstances under which you had me.

If you have a family somewhere and do not want your peace to be interrupted, spare a thought for a woman who feels incomplete until she sees you. I am not looking for you to share whatever you may have made and bequeathed to your children in that family. By the grace of God, I have enough to satisfy me, my daughter and those God has put under my care. If, because of your status or present circumstances, seeing you should be a secret that only the two of us would share, I'm prepared to grant you that anonymity.

I can't wait to hug you and ask you about all the gaps in my life. I need to fill those gaps. I need closure. And you are crucial to bringing me the much-needed closure.

Kindly reach out if you read this letter and know you possibly could be the one I'm writing to.

Yours sincerely,

Yvonne.

Acknowledgment

Mother: Thank you for giving me a second thought and keeping the pregnancy. Thank you for enduring the pain of birth. Thank you for taking care of me the best you could and, most importantly, giving me the best education you knew at the time.

My fans: I am all I am today because of you. Today, I tell my story to you. I hope it's worth reading. Thank you for loving and supporting the YN Brand from the very beginning. We have grown together. Say hello anytime. Let's have a chit-chat some time.

Maanan Akoubor: You came into my life at the perfect moment. We only look back to see how far we have come. Thank you for being so true and genuine. Thank you for stepping in for me when I had no one.

Francis Addo: Brother, I love you now and forever. You mean so much to me. You are a man of little words but big actions.

Sylvia Davies: Sis, we've had our differences since we were kids, but I'm happy we are in a good place now. Thank you for your support. I love you and Nana so much.

Karen Boateng: My special good luck charm sister and friend, I'm glad after 2 decades, we still get the time to giggle and share our old SSS jokes. Thank you for believing in me and getting me here. I AM HERE BECAUSE OF YOU. I love you so much.

Fianko Bossman: My high school boo, thank you for everything. Thank you for helping me start JLM and being that brother to me. Besties forever and ever. Amen!

Afari S. Dartey: You inspire me daily. Thank you for being brutally honest about life. You teach me every day. It has toughened me up.

Abdul Salam Mumuni: Alhaji, what you saw in me is still at work!. Thank you for the opportunity.

Kelvin Kobiri: Thank you for entrusting me with money in 2011 to produce my first-ever movie, The Price. I am producing today because you believed in me.

Felix Anaman: You are a friend I wish I had met earlier. You are one of a kind. Your talent and attention to detail are out of this world. I am proud to be in your life.

Sammy Forson: Brother, I miss the friendship. We can do better.

Kwabena: You have your own way of empowering people. You surely touched me in a powerful way. Thank you. God bless you.

YN Productions: Liebe Ametewee, Peter Avettey, Junie Annan, Bernie Anti and Celestina, thank you. You are a magical team. Without you, I couldn't have achieved all the successes.

Manasseh Azure Awuni: To a man I respect so much, thank you for being a pillar and an inspiration.

Majid Michel: You have been the most real. You were nice to me on my first day on set and that said a lot about you. I have so much to say, but the world already knows how I feel about you. I hope you know too. Love you, bro.

Prince David Osei: Brother, what we share is beautiful. I appreciate you. Thank you for always looking out for me. Love you.
Dr. Mawuko: Thank you for the encouragement and push to pursue higher education.

Simon Rothmund: You're an exceptionally special human. You are truly rare. I pray God grants you all your wishes.

Johnson Kotey: Thank you for saving my daughter's life. You were my angel when my water broke. I can never forget you.

Dr. Kwesi Adjabeng: Thank you for being so selfless. There aren't many of your kind left in this world. Your love for the word of God is everything. You are an angel.

Dr. Luitgard Darko: Thank you for being so good at what you do. Meeting you has been life-saving.

Dr. Kojo Ahor-Essel: Thank you for always making the time. I appreciate you and all you stand for.

Dr. George Arhin: I'm lucky to have you in my life. I hope I inspire you to achieve all you wish for. ["This remembers me," in TIC TAC's voice].

Peggy Ohene Agyekum Boateng: We started Just Like Mama together as an employer and employee, but time has its own way of beautifying authentic connections. You are a sister now. Continue making me proud.

JLM: To a team I hold dear to my heart, to you who helped start the business, to you who left the business, and to you who are with the business, I say thank you so much. You all have contributed and helped shape this institution to be one of the best educational facilities in Ghana.

Printed in Great Britain
by Amazon